AF269408

DANIEL

OTHER
BIBLICAL CHARACTER STUDIES
BY WALTER C. KAISER, JR.

The Lives and Ministries of ELIJAH and ELISHA

ABRAHAM The Friend of God

JOSHUA A True Servant Leader

The Journey from JACOB to ISRAEL

JOSEPH From Prison to Palace

NEHEMIAH The Wall Builder

THE TWELVE The "Minor" Prophets Speak Today

ZECHARIAH The Quintessence of Old Testament Prophecy

SAMUEL The SEER First In The Prophetic Movement In Israel

DANIEL The Man Highly Esteemed By God

JUDGES When Times of Peace or Judgment Reigned

RUTH & ESTHER Women of the Providence of God

— ✡ —

COMING SOON

EZEKIEL Study of Israel In The Last Days

DAVID A Man After God's Own Heart

MOSES The Man Who Saw the Invisible God

SOLOMON The King with a Listening Heart

DANIEL
The Man Highly Esteemed by God

Walter C. Kaiser, Jr.

Lederer Books
An imprint of
Messianic Jewish Publishers
Clarksville, MD 21029

Unless otherwise noted, all Scripture quotations are taken from the New American Standard Bible. Nashville: Thomas Nelson Publishers, 1978; the Complete Jewish Bible, Baltimore: Messianic Jewish Publishers, 1998; or the New International Version Bible, New York: International Bible Society, 2002.

Cover design by Lisa Rubin, Messianic Jewish Publishers
Graphic Design by Yvonne Vermillion, MagicGraphix.com
Editing by George August Koch

Cover art by Gustave Doré, an Alsacian artist, most famous for his depictions of numerous scenes from the Bible.

ISBN: 978-1-951833-18-3

Printed in the United States of America

Published by:
Lederer Books
An imprint of Messianic Jewish Publishers
6120 Day Long Lane
Clarksville, MD 21029

Distributed by:
Messianic Jewish Publishers & Resources
Order line: (800) 410-7367
lederer@messianicjewish.net
www.MessianicJewish.net

DEDICATED TO
these wonderful friends
who met to study the book of Daniel
every Tuesday afternoon and blessed all of us.
May our LORD richly bless each of you!

Joel & Christel Bastian
Tom & Denise Flickinger
Roger & Nancy Gosse
Fred Heinz
Bill & Laurie Helmke
Nancy Hilbelink
Nancy Kaiser
Paula MacDonald
Linda Mursau
Tom & Sue Rice
Rick & Rhonda Roesch
Joan Rothwell
Linda Schilling
Jon & Cindy Scott
Wayne Uglem

Table of Contents

Lesson 1

Knowing Where and When to "Draw the Line"

Daniel 1:1–21

Introduction

Few books of the Old Testament are as hotly contested as Daniel regarding date, authorship and even some analysis, though it is easy to interpret. However, on its own, the book does pose at times a unique set of characteristics: for example, it is written in two languages (Hebrew and Aramaic), and it is narrated in two voices (in the third person generally for the *court stories* of Daniel 1–6, and first person usually embedded in third-person narration of the *visions* in Daniel 7–12).

But there are several other issues that face the interpreter of this book. For instance, there are two basic positions in the dating of this book: one is labeled the "traditional" view, which understands the book as a *sixth century* B.C.E. *composition written by the prophet Daniel*, and the other view is labeled the "critical" or "mainline" interpretation, which sees Daniel as a late *second century* B.C.E. work. The latter group say the "traditionalists" fight what some regard as a "rear-guard action," when they defend Daniel's historical reliability and argue for a more conservative, earlier sixth-century date. However, the voices of many conservative scholars, such as E. J. Young, K. Kitchen, D. J. Wiseman, and J. G. Baldwin continue to present an extremely good case for the traditional view, a sixth-century date, and a genuinely prophetic interpretation.

In most centuries past, traditional Jewish and non-Jewish scholars ascribed the book of Daniel to a Hebrew author, who was taken captive in Judah by King Nebuchadnezzar in 605, and who continued serving in the royal courts of Babylonia and the Median-Persian Kings until at least 536. This set of circumstances came about as the result of a high promotion given to this man, and to his three Hebrew friends, who were taken captive from Israel.

Even though the Neoplatonist author Porphyry (233–304 C.E.) was critical of the historicity and the date usually given to this book, Porphyry insisted a 2nd century B.C.E. writer reported the history in his book as if it had been spoken much earlier in the previous centuries. As a result, modern critical scholars began to take the same line of argumentation, beginning especially in the late nineteenth and early twentieth centuries. Today, that same line of specious reasoning is found among all too many who claim to be biblical scholars, and lately, even among a few evangelical scholars and ministers. However, the historic details of the book, including its chronological accuracy and its prophecies, have been shown accurately to reflect a large part of the culture and times of the sixth century B.C.E. Moreover, in case after case, the future events it talked about were fulfilled as if they had been spoken centuries ahead of time, for indeed, those events had been composed in the sixth century B.C.E. though fulfilled centuries later.

Structure of the Book

That the book is in two languages, Hebrew (1:1–2: 4a; 8:1–12:13) and Aramaic (2:4b–7:28), points to the fact that Daniel addressed his own people in their native Hebrew tongue at the beginning and end of his book, while also addressing the Gentile nations in the central section in their Aramaic language, the *lingua franca*—or the tongue of international commerce and trade of the day. This linguistic distinctiveness, then, becomes an interpretive clue as to whom Daniel was primarily addressing in his messages: He had a word for the Gentiles in the Aramaic sections, and a word he highlighted for the Jewish people in Hebrew sections. Moreover, the chiastic arrangement of the subjects treated in the Aramaic section from 2:4b to 7:28 give further evidence of this bifid structure (a.b.c. c.' b.'a.') within this book. That chiastic structure would look like this:

a. Four World Empires Will Be Replaced by the Kingdom of God – 2:4b–49

  b. Suffering Will Come Via the Threat of the Fiery Furnace – 3:1–30

    c. Daniel Interprets Nebuchadnezzar's Dream – 4:1–47

    c.' Daniel Interprets the Handwriting on the Wall – 5:1–31

  b.' Suffering Possible from the Threat of the Lion's Den – 6:1–28

a.' Vision of Four World Empires Will Be Replaced by the Kingdom of God – 7:1–28

Theological Emphases

The book of Daniel is governed by a "Theology of History," in which the person and work of God the Father and Jesus the Son of Man remain in charge of all events and all nations, even though the Israelite exiles have been dealt an intense shock in the violent sack of Jerusalem. But the Promise-Plan of God was still operative, despite the strangeness of a new land, strange customs, pagan culture, and idolatrous religion in Babylon. God's promises were still "irrevocable" (see Rom. 11:29). God still owned the land of Israel, where his covenant with the patriarchs and David was still in full force, for he was God of gods, Lord of lords, and the Decider of the destiny of all the nations.

There will be more opportunity to expand on these points when we take up each of the chapters in Daniel, but it is time to get into the text itself. The first chapter calls us to "draw the line" ethically, morally, and theologically today just as Daniel and his friends were called to do.

The Character of Daniel

Daniel, meaning "God is my judge," wrote what is regarded as the last of four major books on prophecy. He is seen in Scripture as a prophet in the sense that Abraham was a prophet (Gen. 20:7) and as Moses was (Deut. 18:15). But Daniel did receive several messages from God even though his main work was that of statesperson. He does not appear to have preached any sermons to the people of Israel in the manner of Isaiah or Jeremiah. Because Daniel did not exercise the gift of a prophet in the usual way, that is why in the order of the books of the Bible in the Hebrew canon, his book was not included with the prophets.

Daniel was taken as a captive to Babylon by Nebuchadnezzar with other Judeans in 605, notably with his three Jewish friends, Shadrach, Meshach, and Abednego, where they were given a secular education for three years. Daniel was born into an unknown family of Judean nobility prior to King Josiah's reformation in 621.

Daniel functioned as a wise man during the early years of King Cyrus (6:28) and continued into his senior years. The last recorded event in his life that is recorded is in the third year of Cyrus (536) when he saw the vision of the conflict between the archangel Michel and the demonic powers of society.

When Others Just Plain Give Up – 1:1–2

The book of Daniel opens with the first of six narratives in the opening six chapters of this book come from life in the royal court of the Babylonian Empire (Dan. 1–6). It relates the story of Daniel and his three friends, who were carried off into captivity from Judah to Nebuchadnezzar's capital court in Babylon in 605/606. The Judean king, Jehoiakim (609–597), who had replaced his father (the noted young and God-fearing good King Josiah), had just recently been installed as a "puppet king" by Pharaoh Necho of Egypt (2 Kgs.

23:30–34). But by the third year of Jehoiakim's reign, Nebuchadnezzar had laid siege to Jerusalem and had carried off with a good deal of the treasures found in the Temple of the Lord in Jerusalem as well as from the Judean palace. Thus in 605, Nebuchadnezzar took Daniel, along with his friends, Hananiah, Mishael, and Azariah (1:6), as captives from Jerusalem into exile in Babylon. This date of the third year of Jehoiakim agrees with the accession year method of reckoning time in Babylon (computing the first full year of one's kingship as beginning with the new year's day after the king had ascended to the throne).

Some critical scholars say there is a chronological discrepancy in the biblical record: Jeremiah 25:1 declares the first year of Nebuchadnezzar's reign is the "fourth year" of Jehoiakim's, not the "third year" as Daniel 1:1 states. But Jeremiah's date is based on the non-accession-year principle (starting to number the king's years from day one of his reign, regardless of where it occurs in the calendar year[1]).

Others worry about the historical veracity of this 605 B.C.E. incursion into Judah, as there is no separate account of a Babylonian invasion into the land of Judah on that date. But even in this case there is indirect evidence of a Babylonian campaign into Judah in 605, for the Jewish historian Josephus, in *Contra Apion* 1:19, cites a Babylonian priest-historian, Berossus, who claimed Nebuchadnezzar was engaged in campaigns in Egypt, Syria and Phoenicia at the time his father, Nabopolassar, died. An additional piece of evidence is now supplied by a cuneiform tablet found in 1956 that Nebuchadnezzar had "conquered the whole area of the Hatti-country" shortly after his Battle of Carchemish in 605. The term "Hatti" embraced the whole of

---

1. Donald J. Wiseman, *Nebuchadnezzar and Babylon*. Oxford: Oxford University Press, 1985: 16–18.

Syria and Palestine. Thus, the report of an incursion is highly likely accurate.

In Times of War and Conquest

All too many tend to argue that in times of war and national distress, the normal way of life is forfeited, or it is seriously infringed on. Ethical decisions are no longer made on the bases of right and wrong, for the feeling seems to take over that most everyone is going to die anyway; so why not live life up to the hilt and forget about divine standards and acting in responsible and moral ways as each was taught to live in the Torah.

The tragic events of the death of godly King Josiah, killed at Megiddo by one of Pharaoh's soldiers in 609 B.C.E., followed by the king of Babylon's invasion of the country in 605 and again in 597, and finally the total destruction of Jerusalem in 586, provided a feeling of despondency for those who despaired of life as they had known it, and might otherwise have called for a change in their faithfulness to God. How was God going to be able to work out his purpose in history and in the life of the nation Judah now that tragedy had struck the heart of the nation these three times? How could the glorious day of the new David, featured at the coming of Messiah, be effective now that the Temple was gone? Did that not mean that the Davidic king would soon be gone as well, and all would now run counter to God's ultimate triumph over evil? Wasn't this so? Or had something important been missed?

In Times of Exile and Questioning

The siege of Jerusalem in 605 would be the first of three major invasions into the land of Judah. Verses 1–2 do not say there was armed conflict, just that the country was "besieged," suggesting more of a threat of a battle. The Judeans thought it the better part of wisdom at this time to hand over the valued articles of gold and silver from the Jerusalem temple and palace and in this way pacify Nebuchadnezzar.

Later, when Nebuchadnezzar was able to check the disloyalty of his Judean vassal, King Jehoiakim, he returned to Jerusalem, after being temporarily preoccupied with revolts in other parts of his empire. But by the time he reached Jerusalem, Jehoiakim had died and his son, Jehoiachin, had been made king in Jerusalem (2 Kgs 24:8). However, Nebuchadnezzar deposed Jehoiachin and exiled him, along with 10,000 Judeans, to Babylon. This time the captives included the prophet Ezekiel (2 Kgs. 24:10–17; Ezek. 1:1–2) in 597 B.C.E.

The third time the Babylonians invaded Judah, Nebuchadnezzar's patience had been exhausted as he initiated a long siege on Jerusalem beginning in 588. Finally, the city fell in 586, the Lord's Temple was razed and burnt to the ground, and the highly esteemed Davidic kingship in Judah was ended—at least for the time being (2 Kgs. 24:18–25:21).

"The LORD delivered Jehoiakim king of Judah into [Nebuchadnezzar's] hand" (1:2). So instead of this being a random event, what happened was not the work of the Babylonians; it was, as it always was, under the aegis of God's sovereign rule over all. The Hebrew verb rendered "delivered" is from the verb for "to give," which appears in each of the three scenes narrated in this chapter: v. 2 ("the LORD delivered [*'gave'*] Jehoiakim king of Judah into his hand"), v. 9 ("God had caused the official to show [*give*] favor"), and v. 17 ("God *gave* knowledge and understanding"). Three times God had *"given"* so that all might know he was indeed God and in charge of where history was going.

None of what had happened in this tragic turn of events was a surprise to Judah, for embedded in the Promise-Plan of God were the warnings of the curses that would come (just as surely, on the alternative action, as the promises would take effect if they believed and obeyed) when they turned away from the Lord. The decisive factor for deliverance would be Israel's obedience and faithfulness to God's call on their lives—which is the same decisive factor in our own national history.

When Pressured to Compromise – 1:3–8

Our Spiritual Heritage

The four young Judean captives are identified by their Hebrew names: Daniel ("God is my judge"), Hananiah ("God is gracious"), Mishael ("Who is like God?") and Azariah ("God has helped"). They were from "the royal family and nobility" (1:3). Note that all four had theophoric names; i.e., they were all compounded with God's name plus a verb or noun), showing their strong commitment to the Lord by their families as well. Surely that indicates a godly heritage and upbringing while they had lived in Jerusalem, and that would stand them in good stead for the years they were torn away from family, nation, and land.

These young men stood out in other ways as well. Their natural good looks and general physical prowess suited them well for leadership positions in the civil service of Babylon. Furthermore, they had "an aptitude for ... learning, [were] well informed, [and were] quick to understand" (1:4). The four were turned over to "Ashpenaz, who was chief of [Nebuchadnezzar's] court officials" (1:3), and who was given the oversight of these men with authority to respond to the requests of all those under his tutelage. The name "Ashpenaz" is attested as an Aramaic name in an incantation bowl from around 600 B.C.E. His name may mean "lodging" or "innkeeper," but his title is even more significant in that he could make decisions without appealing to a superior. That independent quality will play an important part in this narrative.

Ashpenaz began his reprogramming and re-education of these four Jewish youths by changing their names. Accordingly, Daniel became "Belteshazzar" ("Bel [i.e., Marduk, the supreme god of the Babylonians] "protects his life"), and the other three became "Shadrach" ("command of Aku" [the Sumerian moon god]), "Meshach" (perhaps "who is like Aku?"), and "Abednego" ("servant of Neg[b]o" [i.e., Nabu, the son of Marduk]. There was little point in objecting to their names, so the Babylonians could call them whatever they wanted; it was not a point on which to take a stand. There were more important matters to be faced.

It was stipulated that their training period would last three years (1:5b). After that, they were to enter the king's civil governmental service. Babylon was also noted for being the center of wisdom. The men would learn the Akkadian cuneiform language (wedge-shaped signs standing for multiple syllabic values), become versed in reading the Babylonian literature, along with the polytheistic worldview that no doubt was contained in the things they were taught. But God protected their minds and hearts even under such terms.

Our Resolve to Remain True

These men were up for the challenges of such an intensive learning curve, but they were not about to say "yes" to any theological or ethical compromise demanded of them. There came a place where they felt they had to "draw a line in the sand" and say they could go no further. Verse 8 declared that "Daniel resolved not to defile himself with the royal food and wine." They deliberately said they could not participate in what was required of them. The Hebrew text reads, "Daniel set his heart not to defile himself." In their case, the royal food posed a problem for Daniel and his friends.

Just what the difficulty with the food was not easily determined, now that we are so far from the culture of that day. We can, however, make several suggestions as to what might have been troubling these

Hebrews. First, the law of Moses prohibited the conscientious Hebrew from eating certain types of food (Lev. 11; Deut. 12:23–25; 14). Since they could not be assured in advance as to what would be given at their meals, this could have been a reason. However, wine was not prohibited by the law, so its inclusion along with the royal food in verse 9 does not make sense as the cause of their distress.

Another cause might have been that the food had been offered to an idol prior to its being served to them. But Daniel and his friends would accept vegetables, which also might have been offered to the idols along with the meat and wine. Certainly, Daniel would have mentioned the issue of idols had that been the heart of their objection.

Thus, it must have been that Daniel interpreted the partaking of the royal food as a mark of formal allegiance to the Babylonian king, whereas Daniel's friends show later in the narrative in chapter 3 that they accepted only the lordship of God and not that of the Babylonian king! However, even this reason is not as clear as it might at first seem, for Daniel and the other three accepted the vegetables. That would lead us to refine this argument and say that the four Hebrews wanted this "trial by vegetables" to demonstrate to the king that their physical stamina and appearance was due to the miraculous work of God and not the quality or the power of the royal food provided from the Babylonian palace. These men wanted it known that their reliance was on God for their nurturing and support even though some might wrongly conclude that God was no longer effective, since he had not kept these Hebrews from the horrors of captivity and subjection to a foreign political power.

This is an interesting case of how to relate our commitments to the Living God and yet be minimally involved in the culture. These men did not decide to simply adopt everything in the culture. However, they would make no fuss over the pagan names given to them, or over the studies they had to engage in; in fact, they excelled over all their classmates. But there still was a place where they would draw a line in the sand and say, "We will go no further!" They decided to take a stand that left them dependent on the Lord God alone.

When We Are Pressured to Conform – 1:9–16

It is not always easy to determine what is trivial and what is of crucial importance for one's own testimony. For example, during World War II, the wearing of a yellow star on one's clothing, or the giving of a Hitler-salute during a parade, would not be classified as "trivial" in retrospect, for it signaled respect for the Third Reich and its leadership. Daniel and company accepted re-education, renaming and training in all the Babylonian curriculum, even as Moses did when he was brought up in the palace of Pharaoh, but in this cross-cultural situation he knew he had to draw a line in the sand (much as the United States had to in the First Gulf War for when Iraq threatened Kuwait's freedom), especially when it came to stating the One on whom each placed his dependence. These men resisted the temptation to go along with the crowd. They took a stand as every believer must likewise take a stand for the Living God!

To demonstrate that God was still at work on behalf of these non-conforming men, for the second time the text says in verse 9 that "God had caused the official [Ashpenaz] to show favor and sympathy to Daniel." Thus, God was not only demonstrating his rule over nations; he was also providentially ruling in the lives of these individuals as well. Therefore, just as earlier in Israel's history, Joseph "found favor" in Pharaoh's eyes (Gen. 39:4), and later in Israel's history, Esther "won … favor" with the king in her royal beauty contest (Est. 2:9), so Daniel and his friends found the same limited concessions to be true here. God's divine intervention on behalf of individuals is just as much part of this story as it is in his rule over Judah and the Gentile nations.

A Dare to Compare

The test was to last only "ten days" (v. 12). This may have been a round number, but it certainly was for a brief time in which the suspicions of Ashpenaz's superiors would not be aroused by any defect in their health, yet it would give enough time to observe some positive results. This test was indeed evidence of nonconformity at some level that affected the testimony of these four Hebrew captives.

Notice how careful the men were, so as not to show any open defiance of the king per se, yet they did not buckle-under and comply with most other aspects of the new heathen culture into which they had been cast as captives. Thus, the alternative to sustaining themselves off the king's menu was to feed on a diet of vegetables and water; hence this became a sort of "trial by vegetables."

Daniel asked, "Please test your servants for ten days" (v. 12). After the ten days had passed, Ashpenaz was to "compare [their] appearance with that of the young men who eat the royal food" (v. 13). This would mark the separation of the four Hebrews from the otherwise prevailing Gentile culture. In this way, a "Diaspora theology" emerged as the Hebrews would distinguish themselves from the influences of a Gentile culture as advocated by the Babylonians, Medo-Persians, or Greeks in later years when the scattered Israelites found themselves in exile in foreign lands.

A Result to Acknowledge

God's providential care was evident in their individual lives just as surely as it was seen in his rule over nations. God caused Ashpenaz to show favor (v. 9) to these men as God had in the past shown favor to Joseph, who also "found favor" in Potiphar's eyes (Gen. 39:4), and Esther later "won … favor" with Hegai, as he instructed her how to prepare for her visit with the Persian king (Est. 2:9). God's intervention on behalf of the captives was not a sidelight to the story, but it was the same theme that Daniel had established in his opening verses in this chapter. The four men emerged from their test of trial by vegetables "healthier and better nourished" than their competitors (v. 15). So, Daniel and his friends won their point and demonstrated the providential working of God on their behalf.

When Pressed to Produce – 1:17–21

Human Wisdom

For the third time in this text, it is emphasized that it was God who once more "gave" (v. 17) something—this time "knowledge and understanding of all kinds of literature and learning." "Knowledge" pointed to academic learning and "understanding" suggested both an aptitude for study and an insight into exercising sound judgment in what they were learning. Here was living proof of the fact that "the fear of the LORD is the beginning of knowledge" (Prov. 1:7).

Spiritual Discernment

When it came time for the Hebrews' graduation, all four were found to be "ten times better than all the magicians and enchanters in his whole kingdom" (v. 20). The number "ten" is no doubt used here as hyperbole, rather than an exact mathematical score (cf. Gen. 31:41; Num. 14:22; Neh. 4:12). But the impression they made was certainly clear enough to merit introduction into the king's civil service, for each received an administrative appointment in the "king's service" (v. 19). Out of the mercy and goodness of God, these men so excelled their classmates that they beat the other apprentices in the Babylonian arts and sciences as they chose to depend on God and not on the occultic arts of the non-gods and certain demonic teachings found in the Babylonian religion and used by the other classmates who were magicians and enchanters.

A final note appears in verse 21 illustrating the "staying power" of Daniel, for he came to his royal office in Babylon under King

Nebuchadnezzar and remained in the office even after the government changed into the hands of another foreign power, the Medo-Persians, in the first year of King Cyrus in 539/8 B.C.E. This meant Daniel held his office in that government for over sixty years, in the royal courts of Babylon and Medo-Persia. His longevity outlasted the Babylonian Empire and extended to the first king of Medo-Persia. Surely, God is the one who is sovereign over men and nations all over the world.

Conclusions

1. God can be trusted even when the circumstances turn sour and not exactly what we would have pre-planned for our lives.
2. To those who are faithful to their Lord, he has the power to grant knowledge, understanding and the ability to use that same knowledge wisely.
3. Daniel 1 is about how God can work both within the lives of a few individuals as well as he can work in the history of nations.
4. Are our inner convictions strong enough to overcome the outer pressure to compromise and to conform to a hostile culture?
5. There is immense value in pledging ourselves in advance to God and his Kingdom so that we act on principle and not just impulsively.
6. When taking such principal stands, we must do so gently, courteously, and appealingly to win over the opposition rather than being merely confrontive in our stand.
7. Those who honor the Lord will be like a tree planted by the stream of water (Psalm 1:3) outlasting even whole empires.

Questions for Discussion or Reflection

1. Is it possible to be a certain part of a culture without being wooed into the trap of adopting it wholesale—especially when it deviates in theology or ethics from what Scripture instructs us?
2. Must all believers draw a line in the sand at one point or another if they are to remain true to their Lord?
3. What are some examples of what is consequential and what is not in the culture that surrounds us today?
4. Can believers so exceed in their studies and lifestyle that they can outdo their unbelieving competition?
5. Does this chapter make a case for those who argue that being a vegan is biblical?

Lesson 2

Facing Our Fallen Culture

Daniel 2:1–49

Daniel 2 is one of the most important, most pivotal chapters in the Bible for understanding its eschatology. It is also one of the longest chapters. It takes place in the "second year" of Nebuchadnezzar's reign (2:1), so we are somewhere between April 603 and March 602 B.C.E.

The story revolves around a troubling dream King Nebuchadnezzar had. There are five scenes in this chapter: (1) the king's dream brings a crisis—especially for the royal wise men (2:1–13); (2) Daniel intervenes on behalf of the wise men to ask God for the meaning of the dream (2:14–23); (3) Daniel is able to describe the dream (2:24–35); (4) Daniel explains what the dream means (2:36–45); and (5) the king responds to Daniel's interpretation (2:46–49).

Nebuchadnezzar was not the first monarch to receive a divine revelation from God by way of a dream. In an earlier day God spoke to the Philistine leader Abimelech (Gen. 22) and to Pharaoh through a dream (Gen. 22; 41), and later, to Pharaoh Neco (2 Kgs. 23; 2 Chron. 35; 2:46–49). But let us look to Daniel 2 to see what this dream means.

Of Our Ultimate Questions – 2:1–13

What Does the Future Hold?

The Aramaic-language section of Daniel begins in 2:4b, just after Nebuchadnezzar told his advisors he had a troubling dream, and is used up to chapter 7. In the chiastic structure, this second chapter of Daniel will be balanced off with chapter 7, as both chapters speak of four successive earthly empires, followed at last by the in-breaking of

God's everlasting Kingdom. The use of the *lingua franca* of that day, Aramaic, is an interpretive tool that shows that these prophecies in chapters 2–7 were addressed primarily to the Gentile nations, rather than to Israel.

Where Is History Taking Us?

The plotline of this court narrative takes place on two levels. First, on the human level, there is the king's challenge to his royal advisors to explain and interpret the dream. Secondly, on the spiritual level, there is another contest between the Living God and the dead idols of the Babylonian pantheon to see if they can do the same—but without any interpretive results, for they are inert "nothings." Earlier in the eighth century B.C.E., the prophet Isaiah had challenged those same idols to do more than just stand like a pile of lumber and a load of stone without a single action; they were to speak and say something one way of the other, either good or bad, if they could (Isa. 41:21–24; 47:9–10; 48:5), so mortals could know if they were alive and real.

Daniel and his three friends had been under the instruction of the Babylonian wisdom-guild for wise men for three years (1:5). Whether this was three full years or is hard to say; their first year was a partial one (e.g., an accession year that did not start until the new year began). But Daniel and his three friends, whether they had graduated by this time or not, stood just as "condemned" as the rest of their class of royal advisors; all who were unable to tell the king what his dream was about would be executed. Yet Daniel and friends too had been trained in the same literature, lore, and culture as the rest of the Babylonian wisdom class. These Jewish men were among those professionals who were designated "magicians," "enchanters," "sorcerers" and "astrologers" (also called "Chaldeans"). But they were to manifest a key difference from their classmates, for they also claimed to be servants of the Most High God!

Does Anyone Know What's Really Going On?

The way these alleged Babylonian experts in dreams operated was that for them, all dreams followed certain laws, so once these wise men were given sufficient data on the dream, its meaning could be uncovered, using the large Babylonian dream manuals available to them. We have recovered from archaeological sources several such dream-manuals. However, they became inordinately long since they tended to hopefully cover every kind of eventuality.

Nebuchadnezzar had his suspicions about the authenticity of these so-called wise men. He must have thought these "professionals" were impostors with no knowledge of the future, so he set up a test for them, in which he wanted to have the contents of his dream described for him before he would hear their interpretation. This put them at a real disadvantage. When they protested that such a request had never been made by people in their wisdom profession, the king took this to mean they were stalling for time and had conspired to mislead him into hoping the circumstances would change (vv. 8–10). It is also possible that, meanwhile, the king's dream still haunted him, even though he may have forgotten the dream itself, or at least some of the details.

Nebuchadnezzar made no bones about his deep anger over the inability of these so-called professionals to do what they claimed (v. 12) and were hired to do, so a royal decree was issued to put all the wise men to death (v. 13). They were, in his estimation, frauds and fake wizards. From a biblical perspective, they indeed had not stood in the council of the Lord, nor had they heard God's word, so how could anyone have expected them to produce the dreams (Jer. 23:28)? To expect their words to be accurate and truthful was just as silly as comparing wheat grains to chaff. To expect their prognostications to be accurate was like comparing a pile of soaking wet wood to the same as a word from God. God's word was like fire and like a hammer that breaks the rock in pieces (Jer. 23:29). These astrologers, however, had one part of their theology partially straight: They said, "No one can reveal [this dream] to the king except the gods [implying, I suppose, the real God of gods], but such gods do not live among men" (v. 11). However, only the true and Living God would be able to do what the king asked, not these pagan zero-gods who were shameful frauds.

Of Our Lack of Wisdom (2:14–23)

Does the Future Hold a "Mystery"?

Apparently, Daniel and his three friends had not been told of the king's execution decree, for some unexplained reason, nor does this court narrative tell us how Daniel was able to arrange, on such short notice, an audience with the king, when he, along with all the others in his class of pros were under the threat of death (v. 14). He was going to have to hurry if he thought he could save his life or anyone else's.

The commander of the king's guard, Arioch (the same name occurs much earlier in time as a name for the king of Ellasar, perhaps somewhere in southern Mesopotamia; Gen. 14:1), apparently had begun to round up the wise men for their pending fate, when Daniel boldly intervened by asking permission to speak with the king (v. 14). He used "wisdom and tact," which spoke of Daniel's ability to act wisely and to use "good taste," which is precisely what was called for in such a "grave" situation. Daniel asked the king for "time" (v. 16).

Who Knows What the Meaning of the "Mystery" Is?

Then Daniel approached his three friends and urged them to "plead for mercy from the 'God of heaven'" in prayer (a title used 4 times: 2:18–19, 37, 44, as a shortened form of "the God of heaven and earth"; Gen. 14:22) concerning this mystery" (vv. 17–18). Note that Daniel used his friends' Hebrew names this time—Hananiah, Mishael and Azariah—and not their Babylonian names (v. 17).

What the king asked for, Daniel termed a "mystery. The Aramaic word is *raz*, which is used eight times in this chapter (vv. 18–19, 27–30, 47). It is used here with the word "to reveal," which made it a technical term for a divine revelation, a disclosure that went beyond human comprehension. As a Persian loanword, it meant a "secret." Thus, what had been hidden from the professional wise men was now to be made known by the Lord to Daniel in a vision that night (v. 19).

Doxologies to God for Revealing the Future

This answer from the Lord in response to the prayers of the four Hebrews gave vent to their relief and their spontaneous expression of praise in verses 20–24. This prayer is a paradigmatic model for all who have experienced God's amazing answers to prayer. They express deep amazement that they, mere mortals, should be given the privilege of sharing in God's knowledge of the future. The closing lines repeat many of the thoughts of the first lines, beautifully linking the poetry of this psalm of thanksgiving as one. This doxology, like other doxologies (4:1–3, 34–37; 6:25–27) distinctively has a four-fold anthem of praise. God's name is to be praised for his wisdom and power; for overseeing the vicissitudes of world history; for his revealing the deep and hidden things; and for his making known the dream of King Nebuchadnezzar to Daniel. What a great God we and Daniel together serve!

Hope for the Future of Our Limited Power – 2:24–35

Intellectual Limitations

Daniel returned to Arioch with the good news that the executions the king had ordered would not be needed, for the king's dream and its interpretation had been revealed to him (v. 24). Arioch took Daniel to the king with the news that he had found a man from among the exiles from Judah who could interpret the dream. (Some people always want all the credit for themselves!) When the king asked "Belteshazzar" (v.

26) if he could describe the dream and its meaning, Daniel replied, "No wise man, enchanter, magician, or diviner can explain to the king the mystery he has asked about, but there is a God in heaven who reveals mysteries. He showed [you] "what will happen in days to come" (vv. 27–28).

Daniel continued: "As Your Majesty was lying there, your mind turned to things to come, and the revealer of mysteries showed you what is going to happen. As for me, this mystery has been revealed to me, not because I have greater wisdom than anyone else alive, but so that Your Majesty may know the interpretation and that you may understand what went through your mind" (vv. 29–30). This type of wisdom cannot be achieved through reason, conventional insight, or anything like that; it can only come from the Living God. There is no One like the Lord God who can foretell what is to come (Isa. 44:7). Interestingly, Daniel did not say that God had revealed this dream so that the king might know that the Lord alone is God. This disclosure would not lead to his salvation, but one wonders why he would not be so affected that he would have confessed him as Lord without delay!

Try as we may, using human research, group therapy, professional consultation, or even any kind of motivational speaking, we too are unable to say what the future holds unless God makes it known to his servants. Just as marathon runners "hit the wall" during a race, so we too hit the wall in interpretation unless God reveals to his apostles and prophets what we are lacking in knowledge. It is his word and his alone that we depend on hearing in situations like this one.

Revelational Limitation

Daniel now began to unfold the dream. As the king was lying in bed, wondering what would become of his kingdom, he saw an immense statue, such as is usually erected to represent gods or kings, but this one was "awesome in appearance." It took a human form but was extraordinary in size and brilliance. "The head of this statue was made of pure gold, its chest and arms of silver, its belly and thighs of bronze, its legs of iron, its feet partly of iron and baked clay" (vv. 31–33).

As the king watched, suddenly a "rock" was cut out of the mountains, "but not by human hands." It struck the feet, breaking the figure into pieces, which blew away in the wind "without leaving a trace." But the rock that struck the statue "became a huge mountain and filled the whole earth" (vv. 34–35). That the rock had been formed "not by human hands" (v. 34) indicated it originated because of God's own will or decree. This feature of the prophecy recalls Isaiah 41:15–16, where those nations who oppressed Israel would be changed into chaff and blown away. And the fact that the rock became a "mountain" that "filled the whole earth" aligns with the previous predictions that mentioned that the "mountain of the Lord's temple," which pointed to the temple in Jerusalem, would be exalted and raised up in the later days as a place where all the nations would travel yearly to be taught by the Lord and to worship him as king (Isa. 2:2–5; Mic. 4:1–4).

Of Our Hope for the Future – 2:36–49

Rulers Rule by God's Permission

Daniel delivered what no one else could even approximate. He had revealed the content of the king's dream in its exact form; now it was time for this Hebrew captive to reveal the meaning of this royal dream. Daniel pointedly announced: "Your Majesty, you are the king of kings. The God of heaven has given you dominion and power and might and glory; in your hands he has placed humankind and the beasts of the field and the birds of the air. Wherever they live, he has made you ruler over them all. You are that head of gold" (vv. 37–38). Even though Nebuchadnezzar had soared to unheard heights of sovereignty and dominion, still there was someone greater than he, who had bestowed all of this on this monarch. There could be no doubt;

Nebuchadnezzar had enjoyed spectacular unity in his reign (symbolized by the single head), unrivaled in his empire's value (gold) and unprecedented in his lordship over most of humankind, including the animal world and even the birds of the air. He was the greatest human potentate up to that time in human history!

Nations Tend to Become More and More Inferior in Unity, Worth and Divisiveness

Once Nebuchadnezzar's time had expired, deterioration would set in as another kingdom (v. 39) would follow his own, which would consist of a duality and be made of "silver," a less-valuable metal. That kingdom would deteriorate further into a third kingdom, made of "bronze," even lesser in value and worth, and it would degenerate into four separate rulers, only to be succeeded by a fourth kingdom of iron and clay.

True, that fourth kingdom would possess the strength of iron, but it would also be shot through with internal weakness of clay, for just as iron and clay do not easily mix or bond together, so the unity once seen in that head of gold would be impossible for this fourth kingdom to achieve, as it was composed of elements that did not coalesce. These two parts "will not remain united" (v. 43b).

Interpreters agree on identifying the head of gold as the Babylonian Empire, but beyond that, confusion sets in. Some say the chest and arms of silver represents only the Median Kingdom, but that does not adequately account for the fact that there are two arms to this second part, along with the chest. Thus, it fits more naturally, both in history and in interpretation, with the duality seen in the Medo-Persian Empire. This also allows for the third empire, which traditional interpretation says is the Greco-Macedonian kingdom, represented by Alexander the Great, who had conquered the entire known world of his day. After he died, his four generals divided up the once-unified kingdom into four different dominions. The fourth kingdom, then, is the Roman or western empire with both its strength and divisiveness— the iron and clay.

The Kingdom of God Will Erupt Into This Present World System to Last Forever

None of these four kingdoms would last forever, Daniel said. "In the days of those kings, the God of heaven will set up a kingdom that will never be destroyed, nor will it be left to another people" (v. 44). These kingdoms would be crushed by God, whose kingdom—the rock cut from the mountain—would last eternally. What a contrast: Whereas one king and one kingdom had succeeded one after the other, a day was coming when God would establish his Kingdom with a rule and a reign that would never be ceded to any other power, for his would last for eternity. While the preceding kingdoms were overtaken by sound defeat, this fifth kingdom would never be overridden by any other earthly power or unexpected storm.

This narrative ends with Nebuchadnezzar falling on his face in deep reverence before Daniel and his God, whom he exclaimed was "the God of gods and the Lord of kings and a revealer of mysteries" (v. 47). Consequently, Nebuchadnezzar lavished gifts on Daniel and "made him ruler over the entire province of Babylon and placed him in charge of all its wise men" (v. 48). Daniel did not forget his friends; he asked that they too be recognized. So, they were made "administrators over the province of Babylon, while Daniel himself remained at the royal court" (vv. 48–49). Nebuchadnezzar honored Daniel and his friends because of what God had done through them, not because of their own abilities.

Despite Nebuchadnezzar's high praise of Daniel's God, there are no signs in this chapter that he was "converted" to the God taught in the Bible; he merely added recognition of another god to his already crowded polytheistic pantheon.

Yeshua himself is that "Rock" or "Stone," mentioned as the head of that fifth kingdom, which is the Kingdom of God announced by John the Baptist and Jesus (Matt. 3:2, 4:23, 12:28; Mark 9:1; Luke 9:1–2). In fact, Jesus refers to this very same passage in Matthew 21:44, after quoting Psalm 118:22, "the stone the builders rejected has become the capstone." Jesus went on to say, "He who falls on this stone will be broken to pieces, but he on whom it falls will be crushed" (cf. Luke 20:18). The inbreaking of Messiah into history will bring devastating judgment; but it will also bring a rule and reign that will last forever.

Conclusions

1. What is this colossus but the worst, as well as some of the best, of everything in the succession of the world empires in history?

2. Sometimes a religious experience can stimulate an impressive response at an artificial level without touching the depths of our being. Nebuchadnezzar illustrates this very point!

3. Such a response from acting on an impulse of the moment is no substitute for real repentance and faith in God. Even Pharaoh gave glory to God at several points during the plagues, and seemed authentic in the moment, but reneged later.

4. God's Kingdom will triumph over every obstacle or challenge put to it in the history of this world.

5. The mysteries of the government of this world for ill remain in God's hands.

Questions for Discussion or Reflection

1. Daniel and his friends were schooled in the ways of the Babylonian wisdom guild. How did they keep their faith in God active in the days they spent in the high offices of Babylon?

2. Imagine what an enormous impression Daniel's interpretation had on Nebuchadnezzar. What parts of the disclosure gave him reason to cheer, and what parts gave him pause? Did he have enough information that he could have confessed God as Lord?

3. How central in the ministry of Jesus and John the Baptist in the teaching and preaching of the Kingdom of God? How central is such teaching in our day? Why is there such a difference?

4. What kind of success is promised to the Kingdom of God in that future day? In what way will it be an indictment on the earthly rules and reigns we have experienced on earth?

5. What sorts of faults does Daniel predict will afflict the fourth kingdom on earth? Are these faults visible yet in our day? Why is this empire represented as being divided into iron and clay?

Lesson 3

Experiencing God's Deliverance

Daniel 3:1–30

In discussing this narrative, interpreters often focus on the golden image's immense size, the furnace's intense heat, and the three Hebrew captives' deliverance in a metaphorical or mythical manner, rather than treating it as a historical event, as the text has presented it to be handled. As Proverbs 29:25 taught, "The fear of man brings a snare, but whoever puts their trust in the LORD shall be safe." This is why it is very likely the three Hebrew captives may have been the very ones the author of Hebrews had in mind as he listed those Old Testament heroes of the faith as those "who through faith subdued kingdoms, worked righteousness, obtained promises, stopped the mouths of lions, [and] *quenched the violence of fire*" (Heb. 11:34; emphasis mine).

So, Nebuchadnezzar's ragtime band struck up the music, anticipating a hot time for the three Hebrew nonconformists who would end up in the king's furnace—Hananiah ("Grace of the LORD"), Mishael ("Who is like God?") and Azariah ("the help of the LORD"). All three of these Hebrews trusted the Lord implicitly. There is where the focus should be!

The plot spans seven scenes: (1) Nebuchadnezzar decreed that all were to worship the golden image (3:1–7). (2) Three of the Jews were accused of disobeying the edict (vv. 8–12). (3) They were threatened and given a second chance to bow down to the image (vv. 13–15). (4) The Hebrews bravely confessed their faith in God (vv. 16–18). (5) The captives were summarily cast into the furnace (vv. 19–23). (6) The king saw the three men unharmed, and a fourth, the Lord himself, in the furnace (vv. 24–27). (7) Nebuchadnezzar praised God (vv. 28–30).

Usually, it is best to recognize each narrative scene in a sermon, or lesson, with a major point in the message outline for each teaching block, but seven points are too many for most class sessions or sermon times, so this discussion combines the first three scenes and the last three, since they are so closely related.

Our Faith May Be Tested – 3:1–15

Daniel's absence from this episode in the court narratives has prompted discussions as to why nothing is said about Daniel or about him also being asked to bow to the golden image, but Daniel was sometimes ill (8:27), and his office as President of the Learned Societies of his day (2:48) may have excused him from such ceremonies. He may even have been away on an official business trip for the government. Either way, his three Jewish friends were caught in a trap quite possibly set just for them by the other wise men, who had not been able to tell and interpret the king's dream as Daniel had. As a result of Daniel's interpretation of the colossus, some of these wise men may have been opted out of positions of power in the government as they went to the three Jewish captives!

Nebuchadnezzar had made a huge image some ninety feet tall and nine feet wide, set on the Plain of Dura. For those who say this is too high for such a statue, recall the Colossus of Rhodes, built around 300 B.C.E., was fifteen feet taller than this golden image! Others incorrectly charged that the fact that this image was set up in the "Plain of Dura" shows this story was just legend. But three such localities bear the name "Dura" in the archaeological tablets from the Babylonian era. In fact, "Dura" means "an enclosing wall," and it is also used to refer to a rectangular mound some 45 feet square and 20 feet high, as it appeared in one proposed site as a base, or pedestal, for such an image. It is impossible to point to the exact place indicated here, but the name and meaning are well-attested from archaeological references.

By a Hostile Challenge: What God Is Able to Rescue You?

The Greek translation of the Old Testament called the Septuagint (LXX) dated this incident in the eighteenth year of Nebuchadnezzar (borrowing this date from Jeremiah 52:29). Still, all officialdom was invited to the "dedication" (vv. 2–3 use the same word, "Hannukah," meaning "dedication," in the original text (this identical word appears in the Feast of Hanukkah, commemorating the "rededication" of the temple in the time of the Maccabees).

Whether this was a representation of the king himself (inspired by his dream), or an image of one of his gods, is not known. But the ceremony of falling before this image when the music was sounded had the effect of pledging an oath of loyalty to the king, even though it clearly had an aura of worship associated with it.

The role of the herald as a public crier or announcer of all royal edicts and injunctions is illustrated in the times of the Bible. Failure to fall in worship at the proper moment was subject to the penalty of death by being thrown into the flaming furnace (v. 6).

The key statement in this section, therefore, comes from the end of these three scenes, in verse 15, where the king arrogantly asked: "What god is able to rescue you from my hand?" The form of this question is emphatic: *What god—if any at all—is there?* This pointed to the fact that the image may well have been one of a false god, as well as to the fact that Nebuchadnezzar had assumed he had absolute authority over the lives of all those under his control. Judah had heard such vaunted and proud questions previously, such as when the Assyrian King Sennacherib asked Hezekiah, the king of Judah, "Has the god of any nation ever delivered his land from the hand of the king of Assyria?" (2 Kgs. 18:33; Isa. 36:18) Nebuchadnezzar too saw himself just as invincible as Sennacherib. Had he forgotten that only Daniel's God had revealed to him the meaning of the vision he had? This would be no ordinary contest among mortals! He was taking on the Living God!

By a Forced Pluralism or Eclecticism

The new rule was that as soon as the six types of musical instruments began to play (rhetorically repeated, it seems, to create some type of dignity and stateliness to this "dedication" scene in vv. 5, 7, 10, 15, all were to fall and worship this image. There may have been a bit of mischief behind this affair, for "some astrologers (Chaldeans) came forward and denounced the Jews" (v. 8). Thus, the idol-image became the occasion for forcing uniformity among all the people and leveling all faiths into one grand universal pagan scheme. In fact, those bringing the charges especially mentioned the fact that the insubordinates were "some Jews whom you [the king] have set over the affairs of the province of Babylon" (v. 12). It is easy to detect the underlying feelings of envy, jealousy, and competition in these words!

Evil persons may be able to harm our bodies, but God alone has control over both our bodies and our souls. No wonder our Lord warned us not to fear what men can do (Matt. 10:17, 28).

By an Enticement to Sin

This was a test for the three Hebrew captives. Its main feature was an enticement to sin by compromising with the culture. Such testing was not from God, for James clearly taught that God cannot be tempted, nor does he tempt anyone (Jas. 1:13–14). All who yield to temptation are those who are led away by their own desires. It is only when desire has conceived that it gives birth to sin and sin, warned James, when it is full-grown, gives birth to death. My teacher, Robert D. Culver, found three temptations here. They were:

The Temptation to Pervert One's Faith

This temptation played on the naturally healthy desire for a visible manifestation of the Godhead. Philip illustrated that affliction in John's Gospel when he demanded, "Show us the Father and we will be satisfied" (14:8). This same demand appeared earlier in Israel's history when Israel demanded of Aaron, after Moses' prolonged absence, that Aaron make for them a [visible] god, for after forty days of absence they feared Moses was gone forever. Unfortunately, Aaron obliged these complainers' request and made the golden calf as Moses' older brother wickedly announced, "These are your gods, O Israel that brought you up out of the land of Egypt" (Exod. 32:4). What makes polytheism so popular, of course, is it widens our choices and makes few, if any, real limitations imposed on our freedoms. On the other hand, monotheism gives us only one choice; once we make that choice, we must leave all other gods or anything that would compete with the One and only true God.

To Compromise One's Faith

James again warns in 4:4 to beware of forming friendships with the world, for friendship with the world is hatred towards God. This is because we compromise and try to walk two paths simultaneously. Of course, the three Hebrews could have agreed amongst themselves that this golden image was really nothing as far as they were concerned, so it would not hurt them if they went along with the majority will of the people to keep up appearances of persons loyal to the throne. But such an accommodating action would violate the Second Commandment. Deuteronomy 5:8–9 clearly stated that such actions would provoke the Living God; mortals were not to bow down to an idol in heaven above, on the earth, or beneath the earth.

To Conceal One's Faith

Even King Nebuchadnezzar wanted to know from these three men, "Is it true? (v. 14). In a situation such as this one, we, like the three men, must ask: Do we try to conceal what we really believe in such situations, or do we speak what is the truth regardless of the effect it might have? This narrative wants to teach us that there is no other option but to tell the truth—not if we are going to follow the Lord.

Our Answers Should Be Readily Available – 3:16–18

We Do Not Need to Defend Ourselves

The men declared they did not need to defend themselves. This was not the answer of arrogance, but the answer of lives that had been clearly observable and under scrutiny all during the time they had been in Babylon. In fact, there was nothing more to say, for what they had said so far was nothing but what was true. They were confident that the God they served was able to deliver them (v. 17).

Nothing Is Too Hard for God

This principle had been taught when this question was asked in Genesis 18:14, "Is anything too hard for the LORD?" Jeremiah 32:17, 27 repeated the same teaching, "Nothing is too hard / difficult / marvelous / miraculous for the LORD." Zechariah 8:6 raised the point again: "'It may seem too marvelous to the remnant of this people at his time, but will it seem too marvelous to me?' declares the LORD." Jesus had to teach this principle to the father of the boy possessed by a demon: "Everything is possible for the one who believes" (Mark 9:23). Jesus himself laid claim to this same truth in the Garden of Gethsemane: "Father, everything is possible for you" (Mark 14:36).

These three men were sure God was able to deliver them out of the hand of the king and his golden image if that was his will, but their chief concern at that moment was the glory and vindication of God's name and reputation. That had to come before their own welfare!

Faith Must Show Four Elements

Even if God's will and action in this case might be different than they hoped, their obedience would not be contingent on God's answering their prayers in the way they hoped would favor them. While 100 prophets of the Lord were spared by Ahab's Secretary of State, Obadiah, in the days of King Ahab and Queen Jezebel (while Jezebel killed off many prophets of the Lord), neither was the godly prophet Uriah spared from being executed even though God spared Jeremiah (Jer. 26:20). Again, even godly James, our Lord's half-brother, was not spared from King Herod's sword, yet Peter did experience his own deliverance at least on one occasion (Acts 12:2). Herein lies part of the mystery of God (Deut. 29:29). Why does God rescue some and not everyone of his own all the time? The answer lies in the mystery of his perfect will—which, when we see our Lord, will become plain for all to see.

The faith of these three men, however, did exhibit four key elements:

True Faith Has Full Commitment in Our Lord

These men saw no need for further talk. They were not choosing their words carefully to escape by virtue of their wordsmithing (v. 16b). Instead, they were fully committed to the Lord regardless of the outcome of the trial they would be forced to undergo.

True Faith Has Full Confidence in God

This did mean, however, that they had no reservations on God's ability to save them, or to be with them even during the fiery furnace (v. 17). To deny God's omnipotence was to deny his very existence. How could God be any less God than the One who could act in such a situation as this?

True Faith Has Full Resolution Regardless of the Consequences

These three Hebrew captives were determined to disobey the command to worship the golden image, no matter what consequences they might incur. They resolutely affirmed, "Even if [our God] does not [rescue us], we want you to know O king, that we will not serve your gods or worship the image of gold you have set up" (v. 18).

True Faith Has Full Knowledge of God's Abilities

As Hebrews 13:6 says, "The Lord is my Helper, and I will not fear what man shall do to me." Their understanding of who God was did not rise or fall on any one incident that may not for the moment have seemed to fall within an expected deliverance pattern. God would still be God, and his will would still be the one that was being worked out.

Our Persecutors Must Acknowledge God's Deliverance – 3:19–30

Despite Their Anger

Nebuchadnezzar was angry in v. 13, but that anger increased in v. 19. Now it became almost irrational as he ordered the furnace made seven times hotter than usual (v. 19), then told "some of the strongest soldiers in his army to tie up Shadrach, Meshach and Abednego, and throw them into the blazing furnace" (v. 20). It is not clear why he wanted a show of this sort of strength, unless he was now fearing there would be a show of divine force on behalf of these men. The captives' boldness was beginning to get to him! But the fire was so intense that the flames, leaping from the furnace, killed the strong men who tossed the three into the super-heated furnace (v. 22).

Despite Their Unbelief

Amazingly enough, the more Nebuchadnezzar persecuted, the more he confirmed the witness of the three Hebrews. When the captives fell into the scorching fire (from an elevated position near the oven), tied up and bound, the king could hardly believe his eyes. Instead of three men in the furnace, he now counted four (v. 24)! To make sure his eyes and memory had not failed him, he asked his advisors: "Weren't there three men we tied up and threw into the furnace?" Naturally, their response was, "Certainly, O king;" there had been only three! So where did the fourth come from?

Interestingly, it was the king who exclaimed, "Look! I see four men walking around in the fire unbound and unharmed, and the fourth looks like a son of the gods" (v. 25). Surely that must have been a real eye-popper for this otherwise proud monarch who thought he had seen it all. His questions must have come one after another. *How did the men get loose? Why are they not burning up? Why are their clothes not on fire? Why are they walking around in the oven? And who is that fourth one with them? Why does he have an angelic or divine appearance?* The king was more than stumped; he was terrified out of his wits!

Had not the Lord himself promised to be with his people in such circumstances as cited in Isaiah 43:1–2? "Fear not, for I have redeemed you. I have called you [Israel] by name, you are mine. When you pass through the waters, I will be with you. ... When you walk through the fire, you will not be burned, and the flame will not consume you."

That fourth person was no one less than a pre-incarnate appearance of the Second Person of the Trinity (another Christophany). Only the king saw this fourth person, which is fitting, as the king was the one who dared ask whether there was any god who could rescue these men from the fire, or from the edicts given in the name of this king. Now he was the one to realize there was exactly one such God, the One who was now with the three men, who were at this moment walking around in the fire as if it were an afternoon stroll. In the mouth of this royal polytheist, his description of the Messiah he saw in the furnace was more fitting to match the identity of an "angel." His talk showed he lacked knowledge, for he likened him to one from the pantheon of gods—though false gods never showed such power as this! But for those who have read the Scriptures, this One was no one other than the Messiah, the Son of the Living God (Mt 16:16). Too bad Nebuchadnezzar would not cry out like the disciple Thomas, "My Lord and my God" (John 20:28). But for those who were in the furnace, the reality of the presence of the Son of God was affirming by their experience of the real presence of the Son of God.

Despite Oneself

It was now Nebuchadnezzar's turn to act. He approached the opening of the furnace and cried out, "Shadrach, Meshach, and Abednego, servants of the Most High God, come out! Come here!" (v. 26). This is the second time he had been given more than enough reason to drop his idol-worship and worship the true and Living God (cf. Dan. 2:47). And he will be given one more opportunity after he recovers from his insanity (4:34), but there is no evidence that he ever was truly converted.

Royal advisors, satraps, prefects and governors crowded around the three men (v. 27) who had been set for incineration, only to find, as they themselves took note: (1) the fire had not hurt them, (2) their hair was not singed, (3) their robes were not scorched, (4) there was no smell of fire on them and (5) they were unbound (v. 25). The only thing the fire was able to affect was the rope that bound each man.

The trust of these three men and the power of their God really affected Nebuchadnezzar. Involuntarily he rendered praise to the God of Shadrach, Meshach, and Abednego (v. 28). He thought God had sent his "angel" to deliver the men, but he realized these three had trusted in this Lord and they had defied the royal command of a mortal king as they chose to worship only this one God (v. 28c–d).

The king thus decreed that anyone of any nation or language who dared to "say anything against the God of Shadrach, Meshach or Abednego [would] be cut into pieces, and their houses [would] be turned into piles of rubble, for no other god can save in this way" (v. 29). If no one could detract from God's greatness, even though they were pagans, how much more care should God's children take, who unwittingly, sometimes deliberately, steal glory from his majesty and power? Defiance of a Babylonian king was directly juxtaposed with the full trust in the real God. Note, however, which was the more effective!

The king then promoted the three men in the province of Babylon (v. 30). I wonder how that was received by those who had raised the trouble for them in the first place. Had they not hoped they would be gone and some of them would be promoted in their place instead? This is high irony: The people had been gathered to worship the golden image but were treated instead to personally witness how God will personally intervene to rescue those who bow down to him and worship him. Surely this was missions in action in the Old Testament, and in Babylon itself, by three witnesses to the truthfulness of the Lord they served. Thus, once again, all the nations of the earth were blessed by the seed of Abraham (Gen. 12:3). So committed were these three that they would rather suffer death than bow to a false god. Surely the word of their miraculous escape from the furnace got all around Babylon.

Conclusions

1. Our Lord can be depended on to either deliver us or to see that justice is done.

2. We must decide to serve God even if it is not his will to deliver us.

3. By faith we and these men can quench the violence of fire.

4. By faith we and they were loosed from their cords that bound.

5. By faith we and they were comforted in their trials as the strong Son of God stood right beside them.

6. By faith God was glorified and by faith his servants were rewarded as they were willing to be faithful to death and thereby to receive the crown of life (Rev. 2:10).

Questions for Discussion or Reflection

1. After the dream of the colossal image, one would think that Nebuchadnezzar would have been humbled. Instead, he appears to have read himself into the story as the total colossus. What is your estimate of this situation? Were the two events connected?

2. What do you think the point was in having everyone fall? Was it a way of surveying who stood with the government?

3. What part do you think the fear of the Lord played in the decision of the three men to refuse the demand to worship the image?

4. What other biblical stories have similar displays of the miraculous working of God to deliver his own?

Lesson 4

Concluding That "Only God Is Great"

Daniel 4:1–37

This chapter of Daniel is the fourth in a series of six court narratives found in Daniel 1–6. This passage has five main scenes: Nebuchadnezzar's proclamation and doxology (4:1–3); the content of his dream (vv. 4–18); Daniel's interpretation of the dream (vv. 19–27); fulfillment of the dream (vv. 28–33); and an epilogue and doxology (vv. 34–37).

Characteristically, some of the older scholars found the unity of this chapter hard to believe, especially as it shifts from the first-person pronoun in the first 18 verses to the third person in vv. 19–33 and back to the first person in vv. 34–37. But to expect the king's madness to be described by the king himself would be to expect that he could speak in the first person of an embarrassing event. He showed real signs of being mentally affected to the point that many saw him as insane.

This account is not dated in the Scriptures, but based on v. 30, as Nebuchadnezzar proudly struts on the roof of his palace and admires all his past architectural and planning successes, it's fair to say this event took place toward the close of his reign. This monarch ruled from about 605–562 B.C, so the events in this chapter must have come around 570; two years prior, Nebuchadnezzar had ended his long siege of Tyre (Ezek. 29:17–18). However, God gave him the gift of the conquest of Egypt instead of the capture of Tyre, just as the prophet Jeremiah said (43:10; 44:29–30). Also, a fragmentary tablet discovered by archaeologists says it was in Nebuchadnezzar's 37th year [which began about April 23, 568] that he marched against Egypt.[1] It seems our chapter fits right into this period in history.

Nebuchadnezzar himself appears to add a moral to his own story after he had been restored: "And those who walk in pride he [God] is able to humble" (v. 37c). Such a conclusion is not far at all from what the Apostle James taught: "Humble yourselves [men and women] in the sight of the Lord and he shall lift you up" (Jas. 4:10).

But the focal point of the text is the one that is repeated thrice in this chapter: "The Most High is sovereign over the kingdoms of men and gives them to anyone he wishes and sets over them the lowliest of men" (vv. 17, 25, 32). So while the mantra of our day is that our favorite sports team, or whatever else, is "great," this text, as illustrated through Nebuchadnezzar's life and experience, teaches that only God is great!

All God's Actions Show He Is Great – 4:1–3

The narrative related in this chapter really begins back in 3:31–33. However, the chapter divisions made in the thirteenth century C.E. were adopted into the Latin Vulgate Version and used later in the Masoretic Hebrew text and the Greek Septuagint. This present chapter division is preferable to the Aramaic ones, which fail to see the literary structure of the ABBA form, i.e., 4:1–3 (A), English text, matches 4:34–37 (A), which in turn contrasts with the two B forms in 4:4–18 and 4:19–33.

Addressed to All Peoples, Nations, and Languages

Nebuchadnezzar begins by sending an open letter to all who were "in all the world" as a sort of sovereign encyclical or edict to all peoples, nations and languages. In this way, he indicated the

---

1. James Pritchard, *Ancient Near East Texts*. Princeton: Princeton University Press, 1969: 308.

importance of what he had to say while also exhibiting a certain sense of his authority and importance. But there is also a certain humility about it; the letter reflects negatively on his own demeanor and past haughtiness in his kingdom when placed against the divine kingdom of the one true Sovereign. Previously, in 3:4, the king had addressed all the "peoples, nations and men of every language." Now he expanded it to all "who live in all the world" (4:1)—the full scope and reach of his realm. The salutation "May you prosper greatly" (v. 1c) or "Peace be multiplied to you!" is a typical greeting in Aramaic letters. It is also found in some epistles, e.g., 1 and 2 Peter.

Composed of God's Signs and Miracles

Nebuchadnezzar had already experienced enough of the work of God to have brought a change in his heart toward the Lord of the universe. The "signs and wonders" he referred to were not those the Israelites experienced when God delivered them from Egypt. They were those wonderful miracles this king had witnessed, such as the revelation and interpretation of his dream, and the deliverance of the three men from the furnace. It is not that miracles were simply a thing of the past, for God was still showing his mighty power, even before the eyes of this Gentile monarch. These miracles had been performed especially for Nebuchadnezzar and his nation.

Demonstrated in the Eternality of God's Kingdom

The king offers a doxology, both at the beginning of his relating his story (v. 3) and at its conclusion (v. 35). His words are almost identical to Psalm 145:13, "Your kingdom is an everlasting kingdom, and your dominion endures through all generations." However, there is no evidence he was aware of the Psalms, their contents, or any of the other Scriptures of the Jewish people. But his praise for the eternal dominion of God certainly is on the main track of why this chapter might have been included in the Bible, even though it is mostly about the testimony from the lips of a pagan king. This was, in a way, a "public confession" that God had an eternal rule and reign that superseded all other dominions and powers, including those of Nebuchadnezzar himself.

God's Interruption of a Prosperous and Contented Lifestyle Shows That He Is Great – 4:3–18

An Easy Lifestyle

The king continued in the first person reporting and explaining how the circumstance of this dream arose. He began by noting that he was at home in his palace resting "at ease" and luxuriating in all he had accomplished. The two synonyms "contented" and "prosperous" (v. 4) formed one idea (a figure of speech called *hendiadys*), for all his potential opponents had been reduced to submission, including Egypt; there were no real threats to his rule in all the ancient Near East! That was indeed a great accomplishment, given the extent of his rule and the fact that he had none of the modern means of communication such as a phone, nor weapons that could have instantaneously delivered destruction hundreds of miles away, as we have.

A Troubling Dream

The only problem he had in his rule of such a vast realm that extended from India to Egypt was a "dream that made [him] afraid" (v. 4b). Many a monarch would have loved to exchange their list of worries for Nebuchadnezzar's single problem: a dream! How trifling and how small in comparison to what could have been wrong in his empire in his day! In that world and in those times, however, a king's dreams could be very portentous indeed. Thus, this monarch's easy and carefree existence was suddenly shattered. He had to know what this dream meant.

Once again, the king turned to his wise men, including "magicians, enchanters, astrologers and diviners" (v. 7), who previously had failed him so miserably that one wonders why he still turned to them at all; they were nothing but charlatans and frauds. However, Daniel and his three friends had received scholarships to study in the same classes with these so-called wise men, which must have made the rest of the class look either good or bad by comparison.

Disappointingly, these wise men were not able to solve the meaning or interpretation of the dream, which is amazing as they possessed (as we know from archaeology) rather-complete tablets of rules for interpreting of dreams of all sorts. Did they realize it was a negative meaning that would humiliate the king and thus they held back? Whatever the reason, they concluded that they could not interpret this dream.

"Finally, Daniel came into my [the king's] presence, and I told him the dream" (v. 8). Why Daniel was belatedly called, especially given his previous success, we do not know. He was attending to other duties in the empire at the time. However, the king had named Daniel "Belteshazzar, after the name of his god," as he declared: "The spirit of the holy gods is in him" (vv. 8b–c). As Daniel listened to the king describe his dream (unlike in chapter 2, when the king ordered his wise men to tell him what he had dreamt), Daniel was "greatly perplexed … for a time and his thoughts terrified him" (vv. 19a–b).

The king had complete confidence in Daniel: "no mystery is too difficult for you" (v. 9c). Daniel had previously told the king that interpreting dreams was not a gift that was native to himself, but it came to him as a revelation from God (Dan. 2:11).

This time, though, Nebuchadnezzar began to describe this dream that troubled him so. As he watched, he saw a tree in the middle of the land with a height so enormous, it was visible to the ends of the earth. It had beautiful leaves, and its fruit was so bountiful that it fed all, including every creature. The animals found shelter under it, and the birds of the air lived in its branches (vv. 10–12). If all creatures were fed from this tree so no person or animal had gone unfed, this indeed would be a highly effective rule and governance, to say the least!

A Messenger From Heaven

However, as the king watched, "a messenger, a holy one, [came] down from heaven" (v. 13) and ordered in a loud voice, "Cut down the tree and destroy it, but leave the stump, bound with iron and bronze" (vv. 23, 14–15). The hyperboles in this description are numerous: the tree's height was unprecedented; its bulk was massive; branches extended far enough to shelter all the animals and the birds; its leaves were healthy and beautiful; and its fruit was abundant. In fact, the Greek translation (LXX) made this tree even more cosmic and global, adding that even the sun and the moon dwelt in its branches. (The Aramaic text of Daniel does not support those readings.)

Suddenly a "watcher" or "a holy one," which the LXX rendered "an angel," appeared with orders to chop the tree down. Angels, of course, are not effeminate creatures with an impossible number of wings; they are heavenly messengers who perform God's will and carry out his word. As God's lieutenants, they restrain the Prince of the Power of the Air (Satan) and are assigned to specific posts, such as the ruling over the Prince of Persia, or the Prince of Greece. These angels also attend church meetings and are most curious and desire to investigate the precise redemption we mortals experience because of Jesus' death on the cross (1 Pet. 1:12). But the order was clear and succinct: Cut down the tree and destroy it!

The declaration uses the neutral pronoun "it" to refer to the action against the tree, then switches to masculine pronouns such as "him," and "his" in verses 15c–16. This is much like the change that also came in the prophecy against Tyre in Ezekiel 26:12, where it referred by means of a masculine singular pronoun at first for a part of the prophecy to the king, only to change abruptly to a series of masculine plural pronouns. This change of pronoun number indicated a switch from talking about Nebuchadnezzar to an event 200 years or more later that would come in Alexander the Great's day. He would end the Tyre's defense by scrapping the ancient ruins of the land-based abandoned city on the shore of the Mediterranean and dumping them into the sea to form a causeway one-half mile out to the new island city of Tyre, which he summarily captured. This hermeneutical clue in this context in the Ezekiel reference tells us that the tree, as used here, was used figuratively, and had both a past reference as well as a future one.

Not only were the leaves stripped off this tree, but so was its fruit scattered and the animals and the birds forced to desert the arbitral sanctuary the tree had previously provided. Then the dream suddenly shifted from a tree to a human reference, where a male person was to be "drenched with the dew of heaven" and to live with the animals and the plants of the earth (v. 15). His mind would be "changed from that of a man" to "the mind of an animal till seven times pass[ed] by for him" (v. 16). This "verdict" was given for one set purpose: "that the living may know that the Most High is sovereign over the kingdoms of men and gives them to anyone he wishes and sets over them the lowliest of men" (v. 17). Such were the contents of the dream of Nebuchadnezzar.

God's Revelation of the Meaning of the Dream Shows That He Is Great – 4:19–27

The Tree Is the King

Daniel at first was bewildered by the dream as the king recited its contents, but then as he began to interpret it, he politely began, "If only the dream applied to your enemies and its meaning [applied] to your adversaries!" (v. 19c). The truth was, Nebuchadnezzar himself was that tree (v. 22). It was not aimed at his enemies or opponents, but the king himself, for he clearly was that tree in his dream. Trees often were used elsewhere in Scripture as symbols of rulers and/or their kingdoms. For example, the "shoot" from the cedar tree symbolized David's royal house/dynasty (Ezek. 17:22–24), but on another occasion it symbolized the nation "Israel" (Ezek. 19:10). For example, the Pharaoh was regarded as a cypress tree in Eden (Ezek. 31:1–9). So that part of the dream had revelational symbols that had previous interpretive roots.

Daniel, facing the king, needed the same courage the prophet Nathan did when he had to tell David that he was "that man" he had just described in his story of how a rich man slaughtered a poor man's one little lamb to sacrifice for a guest who unexpectedly came to his palace even though he owned many sheep. Over the years Nebuchadnezzar had "become great and strong" (v. 22b). His "greatness had grown until it reached the sky, and [his] dominion extend[ed] to the distant parts of the earth" (vv. 22c–d). Indeed, the Aramaic word for "great," *tap*, appears six times in this passage (vv. 3, 11, 20, 22, 30). However, it will become clear to this king and all others that only God is great.

The Messenger Is From Heaven

As for the "cutting down" of the tree announced by the messenger (v. 24), Daniel avoided the additional words in verse 14 that spoke of trimming the tree's branches, stripping of its leaves, scattering of its fruit, and the mind-change that had been ordered for the man the tree represented. But the essentials of the interpretation were still clearly given Nebuchadnezzar, interpreted Daniel, would be "driven away from people" and would "live with wild animals" and "eat grass like cattle and be drenched with the dew of heaven" for "seven times" (v. 25). The Aramaic word "times," *`iddanin*, appeared in Daniel 2:8; 3:5, 15; 4:16, 25; 7:25 and represented "years," or as it does here, "seven years" (vv. 16, 25). All this is called for by God himself, since Nebuchadnezzar may have become proud, boastful, full of himself, so that God had to bring him low, just as he is able to bring any person low who likewise begins to exalt himself over God (Prov. 29:23).

Patiently God waited for over a year for any change in the king's demeanor; the text said exactly "twelve months" intervened between the night of the dream and its present call for enforcement (v. 29). But one year later, on the very night when Nebuchadnezzar had strutted on the roof of his palace, musing over his enormous success as a ruler, he pompously exclaimed, "Is this not the great Babylon I have built by my mighty power and for the glory of my majesty?" (v. 30) God's judgment swung into action while these very words were still on his lips (v. 31).

There is no doubt Babylon was an enormously wonderful city. It was the largest and finest city in the world in that day. It had eight major gates, including the famous Ishtar Gate on its north side (now removed and reassembled in the Berlin Museum to half its original height). From this gate ran Processional Street for some 1000 yards, decorated on either side with icons of 120 lions and 575 dragons representing the gods Marduk and Bel. Moreover, there were over 50 temples inside the city gates, with the grand temple of Marduk at the end of Processional Street, with its imposing ziggurat called Enemenanki.

Recall that at that time, the Euphrates ran right through Babylon, dividing the city into east and west portions, with a suspension bridge in the middle of the city, 600 feet long and 30 feet wide, while ferries operated across the Euphrates River at the northern and southern end of the city to assist crossings during the daytime. According to the Greeks, the Hanging Gardens of the Babylonian Palace were one of the Seven Wonders of the World, but that fact is often contested as to whether this was the palace the ancients meant. Indeed, Babylon had become an aura of splendor that was rarely seen in the ancient world.

Daniel Calls for a Change and for Repentance from the King

No one can say Daniel did not evangelize to this monarch. Good preacher that he was, he pressed home the precise point: The king should immediately "renounce [his] sins" and "[his] wickedness" and "do what is right" (v. 27). God not only wanted full repentance; he also wanted to see tangible evidence that the king had been changed inwardly in repentance as signaled by outward marks of "being kind to the oppressed" and "[doing] what was right." Some have incorrectly taught based on this verse that sins can be atoned for by good works and almsgiving, as the apocryphal book Tobit incorrectly urged (Tob. 12:9; 14:11; Ecclu. 3:29–4:10). For example, the *Jerusalem Bible* unhelpfully renders this passage in Daniel, "May it please the king to accept my advice: by virtuous actions break with your sins, break with your crimes by showing mercy to the poor and so live long and peacefully." The 1970 Roman Catholic *New American Bible*, otherwise often very well translated, rendered 4:27 as "Therefore, O king, take my advice: atone for your sins by good deeds, and for your misdeeds by kindness to the poor; then your prosperity will be long." This is accompanied by a footnote that states boldly, "A classic Scripture text for the efficacy of good works." Verses such as this one, though, were often at the center of the controversy in the Reformation times as to whether merit could be earned toward one's salvation by good works. The Scriptures and the Reformers were emphatic: Salvation cannot be earned by works.

What's more, to translate the imperative "renounce" (Aramaic *peruq*) as "atone/redeem," as the Latin and Greek translations do, is unwarranted; this meaning never occurs in Aramaic or in the parallel Hebrew word until much later in post-biblical times. Moreover, the actual meaning of this word can be gained from the cognate Hebrew word in Exodus 32:2, where Aaron instructed those who wanted a visible god to "tear away," "break off" or "snatch off" their golden earrings so they could contribute them to building the golden calf. The imagery is one of breaking, releasing or snatching a yoke from the neck of an ox; thus, it has a similar meaning of the act in our responding to the offer of salvation!

In God's Patience With the King, He Is Great – 4:28–33

God Waited Twelve Months for Repentance

Daniel's urgings went unheeded by this proud king for a full year. Therefore, the dream was fulfilled. Surely the lapse of an entire year before God acted in judgment speaks volumes for how long-suffering and patient God is, and that he is not willing than any should perish, but that all should come to repentance. Even as the king was in the very act of boasting about all he had accomplished, God brought about what he had warned might happen if he turned away from this Living God.

God Carries Out His Threat

His demise began with a "voice from heaven" (v. 31). The source of this voice is not identified, but there can be little doubt that it was a voice from God, or from one of his angelic hosts that he had authorized to sound forth the initiation of the divine judgment. But even more to the point, the time for Nebuchadnezzar's sovereignty and authority was to be suspended for a period of seven years, which had now begun (v. 31c). He had brought on himself all this trouble because of his stubbornness to repent and turn to God in humble repentance and contrition.

He was "driven away from [his] people," and he began to "live with the wild animals" (v. 32a). He now ate grass as his food, for such would be his lifestyle until a full seven years had passed (v. 32c). Only then would his senses be restored to him, when he would "acknowledge that the Most High is sovereign over the kingdoms of men and gives them to anyone [God] wishes" (v. 32d).

God's Restoration of the King's Senses Shows That God Is Great – 4:34–37

The King Looks to Heaven

In this last section, as in the initial first three verses of this chapter, the literary form returns to the first-person pronoun narrative. This makes a fine example of the figure of speech called an inclusion, or bracketing, of the whole narrative from start to finish.

Finally, the king "raised [his] eyes toward heaven." Then his sanity was restored as he "praised the Most High" and "honored and glorified him who lives forever" (v. 34).

The extant records of Babylon say nothing about this seven-year hiatus in Nebuchadnezzar's reign. (Near Eastern records rarely if ever noted their losses or any embarrassing negative happenings. It was not good for the king's image and press releases.) For those critics who try to declare this episode mythical, theirs is an argument from silence, and it should be responded to in kind—with silence.

The King Glorifies God

The song of praise sung by the king reminds us of the words in Psalm 145:13, 115:3; Isaiah 40:17, 44:27. Nebuchadnezzar exalted God, "because everything [God] does is right, and [God's] ways are just" (v. 37b). Is this an indication, then, that he was soundly converted?

Furthermore, he amazingly was restored to his throne once again after being away from his royal privilege for seven years. He enjoyed the honor and splendor he and his kingdom had known previously (v. 36). His advisors and nobles sought him out once more, and he possessed all that he had had before this sad event. He even warned others "that those who walk in pride [God] is able to humble"—he surely should be one who knows the truth of that saying! Nebuchadnezzar indeed was a star witness to that very same fact!

Conclusions

1. God can bring down proud nations and haughty leaders in our day just as he has done in the past.

2. We must not substitute the greatness of ourselves, our congregations, or our nations for God's greatness; he will not allow any competition with himself.

3. It is the Lord alone who is great and greatly to be praised (Psalm 48:1).

4. Let us take heed to ourselves and where it is we need to repent and to renounce our sins, for such flamboyance hinders the work of God.

5. We must say to ourselves and shout to the world: "Behold your God!"

Questions for Discussion or Reflection

1. Do you think that the effectiveness of Nebuchadnezzar's early reign could be attributed to God's Common Grace as it came to King Cyrus in Isaiah 45? Are there modern examples of this Grace offered to contemporary rulers?

2. Was Nebuchadnezzar's dream evidence that God cared for the salvation of Gentiles as much as he cared for Jewish conversions?

3. Why do you think God made Nebuchadnezzar's derangement extend for seven years? How was he able to exist in such a lowly estate for such a lengthy period?

4. What is your estimate of Nebuchadnezzar's witness about his experience in Daniel 4:1–3 and again in 4:34–37? Did he accept the Lord as his Savior?

5. Why did God bring this king back to rule again after he had judged him so severely? Is God the God of second chances?

Lesson 5

Honoring the God Who Weighs Our Lives in His Hands

Daniel 5:1–31

The fifth chapter of Daniel continues with another of his six court narratives. The text falls into five different scenes: (1) the celebratory banquet of Belshazzar (5:1–9); (2) The Queen Mother's speech (vv. 10–12); (3) Belshazzar's speech (vv. 13–16); 4.) Daniel's speech (vv. 17–28); and (5) the way the banquet ended (vv. 29–31). All events in this chapter took place in one evening, which also became the last evening this empire lasted, for the end of the Babylonian kingdom came that night in October of 539 B.C.E. It was all over for Babylon.

It all happened within some 32 years of Nebuchadnezzar's death in 562. The Greek historians Herodotus and Xenophon recount how the Persians had dug a trench to divert the Euphrates' upstream waters into a lowland; the natural course of its current would ordinarily run right through Babylon. But when the depth of the water was severely lowered by the Persians creating this bypass, it let the enemy troops enter the city through the depleted riverbed. Unfortunately, the drunken guards and tipsy government officials on duty missed any signs of what was taking place and realized too late what was happening on that final evening of the Babylonian Empire.

Once again, however, mainline scholars treat this chapter in their preferred critical way, alleging it contains a "prophetic legend," a "myth," a *midrash* or *pesher*. Scholars have three issues that they say precludes treating this chapter as historical: (1) the writing on the wall, (2) the lack of a clear identity of the Queen Mother, and (3) the claim that the conquerors of Babylon, and the new victors, were a combination of the Medes and Persians, not just one of the two nations.

But if Daniel 4 was God's final word to Nebuchadnezzar, then Daniel 5 was God's final word to Belshazzar. It became clear God was just as much in charge of the heathen Gentile world, the nations they represented and thought they ruled exclusively, and even in charge of their rulers, as he oversaw the Jewish people. The degeneracy of respect for the sacred vessels of God, stolen from the temple in Nebuchadnezzar's day and now used to toast pagan deities in Belshazzar's, shows how the morality and the fear of God had likewise declined. Indeed, the glory of Babylon was also declining. Nebuchadnezzar's successor Merodach (562–560) ruled for just two years due to his notoriously wicked ways, then was murdered by Neriglissar, his sister's husband. Neriglissar (560–556), in turn, died on the battlefield in the fourth year of his reign. His infant son Labashi-Marduk (556) was enthroned for just nine months when Nabonidus (555–539) usurped the throne at age 60, after he had tortured the young king to death. Most of the last years of Nabonidus' reign were spent in Tema, in the Arabian Peninsula, while his son carried on the affairs of state in Babylon. At least half of Nabonidus' 17-year reign saw him "entrust the kingship [to Belshazzar]," as the archaeological document called the "Nabonidus Chronicle" attests.

Our Response to the Sacred – 5:1–9

Sacrilegious Insolence

After Nebuchadnezzar's death, the glory of Babylon rapidly faded. Yet the nation continued its high ways as if nothing had happened. In fact, Belshazzar, who had taken over the daily operation of the affairs of state while his father, Nabonidus, was living in Tema, Arabia, "gave a great banquet for a thousand of his nobles and drank wine with them" (v. 1). But suddenly the convivial mood of all at the feast turned as Belshazzar "gave orders to bring in the gold and silver goblets that Nebuchadnezzar, his father had taken as booty from the temple in Jerusalem, so that the king and his nobles, his wives and his concubines might drink from them" (vv. 2–3). That is when things got ugly.

Belshazzar defamed and desecrated the God of Israel by using the goblets that had been taken from Jerusalem's temple in 586. What was sacred and had been dedicated distinctly to God was used by the king, his nobles, wives, and concubines as they drank and "praised the gods of gold and silver, of bronze, iron, wood and stone" (v. 4).

Five times in this chapter Nebuchadnezzar is called Belshazzar's "father" (vv. 2, 11, 13, 18), and the latter was called his "son" (v. 22). However, as we know Nabonidus was his real father, let us recall that the terms "father" and "son" are often used figuratively. Elijah was called Elisha's "father" (2 Kgs. 2:12), and their disciples were called "sons [i.e., members] of the prophets." It is possible, though, that Nabonidus married Nebuchadnezzar's daughter and that Belshazzar was thus Nebuchadnezzar's grandson. The term "father" is also often used in Scripture for the more-precise term "grandfather."

Excursus on Drunkenness – Proverbs 23:29–35

Belshazzar's decision to introduce the vessels—taken from God's temple almost fifty years earlier and now handed over to a drunken crowd—must have meant he too was already deeply intoxicated. His father, Nabonidus, may have wanted to offend the four Hebrews who had been in Belshazzar's employ—especially if, as some argue, King Nabonidus was attempting to alienate the Jewish affection for Belshazzar in his comeback to regain the Babylonian throne after being away for some time. The scene was one of ostentatious opulence. It is very reminiscent of the feast sponsored later by the Persian king Xerxes (Est. 1:2–5). Later banquets, such as this one, were noted for their orgiastic and cultic practices, but whether that was true here or not, what happened was revolting to say the least.

We are not told what occasioned this banquet, but given how swiftly events moved that same night, it may have been meant to be a morale booster against the impending invasion of the Medes and Persians. The text specially notes that Belshazzar was drinking "with" (Aramaic *qabel*), or "in the presence of," his nobles. This is most unusual, for normally the king was hidden from the view of the others at the banquet hall. Does this suggest then that he was "showing off" in the presence of his wives and concubines?

Not only was the whole scene immoral, so was Belshazzar himself. His reckless call for the goblets from Jerusalem seems to suggest that he wanted, in his intoxicated state, to blaspheme God by making him to look common and ordinary over against what usually was regarded as sacred. If nothing else, superstition alone would have dictated that such an act of high insolence should be avoided in public.

It is no accident that the warning in Proverbs about drunkenness (23:29–35) is juxtaposed with the warning against the lure of foreign and unfaithful women (23:26–28). Now the charming vixen is placed opposite the charms of the product of the vine. The teaching in v. 29 begins with a riddle expressed in a six-fold repetition of words, "Who has…?" Each question, in a repeated anaphora, is answered in v. 31. While Scripture does not teach total abstinence but moderation, it does warn against drunkenness as a sin (Deut. 21:20–21; 1 Cor. 6:9–10; Gal. 5:19–21).

Praise to the Gods of Gold and Silver

Add to the drunkenness the brash invocation of idol gods, while they are toasting these false deities using the sacred vessels originally dedicated to God, and you have a recipe for a disaster.

Who, then, has "sorrow," "strife," "complaints," "needless bruises" and "bloodshot eyes?" Who indeed—except those who lingered over wine, Solomon taught (Prov. 23:29–31). The consequences of lingering over alcoholic beverages are that one will "see strange sights," "imagine confusing things" and act like one who is "lying on top of the rigging" of a ship (vv. 33–34), unaware of the danger he is in.

Suddenly the revelry was interrupted by "the fingers of a human hand … [which] wrote on the plaster of the wall, near the lampstand in the royal palace" (v. 5). Archaeologists have uncovered a large throne room, some 56 feet wide and 173 feet long, in Babylon. Midway along the long wall, opposite the entrance, was a niche on the front of the wall, covered with white plaster. This may have been the very room and the same wall where the writing appeared. This event was enough to alarm the king as "his face turned pale … and his knees knocked together and his legs gave way" (v. 6). To understand what all this meant, the king called for the "enchanters, astrologers and diviners," who previously had been unable to tell Nebuchadnezzar's dream. Any man who could interpret the handwriting, the king promised, "will be clothed in purple and have a gold chain placed around his neck, and … be made the third highest ruler in the kingdom" (v. 7). This promise of being "third" confirms that Belshazzar himself was second in the kingdom to his father Nabonidus.

Our Response to the Revelation of God's Will – 5:10–16

The Setting of God's Revelation

Alarmed that the wise men were unable to decipher the writing on the wall, the "Queen Mother" entered the hall unbidden on hearing the commotion caused by the mysterious writing (cf. Est. 4:11). She urged Belshazzar to stop worrying and looking so pale (v. 10). This could not be Belshazzar's queen-wife, for his wives and concubines were already at the banquet. Nor could she be the aged widow of Nebuchadnezzar, for whom he built the hanging gardens to overcome her homesickness for the Amytis, the hills of Media. This is the wife of Nabonidus and mother of Belshazzar, called Nitocris, a daughter of Nebuchadnezzar.

The Arrival of God's Revelation

Her solution was to call attention to previous work of Daniel and his gift of interpreting dreams and the like, who "in the time of your father was found to have insight and intelligence and wisdom like that of gods" (v. 11). She refers to "Daniel" by his Hebrew name, for she had lived long enough to have witnessed what he had done in the past.

Daniel was summoned immediately, and his past accomplishments were rehearsed (vv. 13–14). He was told of the wise man's inability to read the writing (v. 15). Daniel was then asked to interpret the writing, and the king told him the gifts he would be rewarded with. Daniel's reply was unexpected: "You may keep your gifts for yourself and give your rewards to someone else. Nevertheless, I will read the writing for the king and tell him what it means."

Our Response to the Lessons of History – 5:17–31

Belshazzar's (and Nabonidus'?) Four Sins

Daniel began his interpretation by reminding Belshazzar, "The Most High God gave your father Nebuchadnezzar sovereignty and greatness and glory and splendor" (v. 18). He was at once feared and dreaded by all nations, for God carried the power of life and death over all (v. 19).

No Humility

As a result of all of God's blessings, the king's heart "became arrogant and hardened with pride" (v. 20a). It was for this reason that God had once stripped Nebuchadnezzar of his throne and sent him away for seven years to live with the beasts of the field until he acknowledged his pride and humbled himself before God.

Excess of Pride

Amazingly, Belshazzar learned extraordinarily little from what his father had gone through. Instead, he had "set [himself] up against the Lord of heaven" (v. 23a). Similarly, the prophet Isaiah had used this same rebuke for the king of Babylon: "You have said in your heart, 'I will ascend to heaven; I will raise my throne above the stars of God. … I will ascend above the tops of the clouds; I will make myself like the Most High' … But you are [now] brought down to the grave, to the depths of the pit" (Isa. 14:13–15). Was Isaiah addressing Nebuchadnezzar or Belshazzar when he made this warning of judgment? It could apply to either one or to both—and did!

Profaned the Holy

Daniel rebuked Belshazzar, noting he had taken the goblets stolen from God's temple and drank wine from them and toasted other gods (v. 23b). The same verb meaning "to profane" also means "to take 'from' [*pro*] the 'temple' [*fanum*]," hence a deliberate act of desecrating or profaning.

Did Not Honor God

"You did not honor the God who holds in his hand your life and all your ways," Daniel said (v. 23d). Because all men and women are made by God in his image, God has a natural claim over all their lives.

The Warning to Belshazzar Via the Writing on the Wall

Names of Weights or Coins?

Because the king had not honored God, that was why "he sent the hand that wrote the inscription" (v. 24), which read, "MENE, MENE, TEKEL, PARSIN" (v. 25). The three terms were not a secret code; the king knew the definition of the terms. Unfortunately, though, scholars have given their own erroneous "solutions." Yet the words are simply the names of three Aramaic weights: a mina, a shekel, and a half-piece. It was as plain as if the writing had said, "a dollar, a dollar, a dime and a penny."

"Numbered, Numbered, Weighed and Divided"

Daniel then interpreted the terms as verbs. He explained: *"Mene*: God has *numbered* the days of your reign and brought it to an end. *Tekel*: You have been *weighed* on the scales and found wanting. *Peres*: Your kingdom is *divided* and given to the Medes and Persians" (vv. 26–28). Belshazzar's kingdom had been numbered in the balances of truth and judgment, and having been weighed, the kingdom would be divided up and given to the Medes and Persians.

Daniel did not mean that the Babylonian kingdom would be divided for the Medes and the Persians to each have a share. Babylon had been placed on God's scales of morality before. The kingdom's rule and reign would pass to the next empire—the Medo-Persian Empire.

That very night, the end came to the Neo-Babylonian Empire. Herodotus, who visited this place 75 years after the fall of Babylon, explained that King Cyrus finished what he had begun in the spring of 539. Though Cyrus had defeated Belshazzar in the field, Belshazzar retreated to his famous walled city of Babylon, feeling that it was so unconquerable that he would be safe inside its massive walls. Alas, as Cyrus had diverted the waters of the Euphrates flowing toward Babylon, so he was able to storm the city through the lowered river, while the banquet was still in progress, so one empire fell as another took over.

In the meantime, Daniel was clothed in purple, given a golden chain, and promoted to number-three in the kingdom for interpreting the writing. However, his promotion was to be short-lived, for "that very night Belshazzar ... was slain, and Darius the Mede took over the new kingdom of Medo-Persia at the age of sixty-two" (v. 30).

Apart from the book of Daniel, the name "Darius the Mede" is unknown to history. This is unusual, since Cyrus is well-known elsewhere in Scripture as the liberator of the Jews from Babylon (2

Chron. 36:22–23; Isa. 45:1; Ezra 1:1–8; 3:7; 4:5; 5:13–6:14). There was a Darius I Hystaspes, who came later in history (522–486), so some think Daniel simply confused the later Darius with Cyrus and incorrectly called him "Darius the Mede." But there are several reasons why this is a poor interpretation. Daniel served in both of those governments at this transitional time, so confusion is most unlikely. Moreover, Darius I served thirty-six years. If he were 62 when he began his reign, that would make him 98 at the end of his reign!

Daniel 6 calls Darius "king" twenty-eight times yet verse 28 equates "the reign of Darius and the reign of Cyrus the Persian." Yet Daniel 1:21 claimed Daniel remained in his old position, one he had been awarded at the beginning of his time in Babylon, with the three other Hebrew captives, and lasted until the "first year of Cyrus."

The fact is, the identity of Darius the Mede remains a historical conundrum to this day. Nowhere outside of the Bible have any of the conservative solutions been verified. Some harmonizers have posed a set of solutions that makes Darius the Mede an alternate name for Gubaru, a district governor who ruled in place of the king—along with several other suggested titles. John C. Whitcomb was one who argued for such a position. However, Donald J. Wiseman argued that "Cyrus the Persian" merely took over the title of "Darius the Mede" for in 550. Media ceased to be a separate nation and became the first satrapy, "Mada." Wiseman translates Daniel 6:28 as saying, "So this Daniel prospered in the reign of Darius, that is, in the reign of Cyrus the Persian." This seems the best solution based on the data we have. Such a solution may be possible, but so far, we have not had outside verification of this dual identity.

Conclusions

1. We must always be cautious about using things that are sacred and dedicated for holy use in a secular or profane way.

2. There comes a time when it is too late for an individual or a nation to respond to the warnings and call of God, for the time for responding to his call has sometimes already expired.

3. God sometimes sends a warning to a nation as a backup to his written Word, but often mortals are so stubborn and bound in their ways that even supernatural events have little or no effect on them.

Questions for Discussion or Reflection

1. How could a kingdom such as the Neo-Babylonian empire last only 87 years (626–539) yet cause such havoc in the ancient Near East?

2. Since we have never documented from history or archaeology "King Darius the Mede," how are to describe his presence in Daniel 5:31? Which solution do you like best and why?

3. What do you make of the method of giving revelation by having a hand write on the wall of a banquet hall three words that could be rendered as three types of coins?

4. What acts of providence can we see operating here in a pagan world? How does its operation among pagans fit your understanding of this doctrine?

5. How God's patience and love seen in his response to the stealing of the sacred vessels from the temple by Nebuchadnezzar?

6. Why do you think Belshazzar did not immediately think of Daniel as the "go-to-person" when he needed an interpreter, but only mourned about there not being such a person despite Daniel's earlier fame in this matter?

7. How would you characterize the character reference the Queen-Mother gave for Daniel to the exasperated King Belshazzar? What stands out in her high praise of him?

8. How can we apply the significance of Daniel's interpretation of the writing on the wall to our nation or to other nations of our day? Are our current caste of rulers, presidents, and generals under a possible similar formal accusation from God if they too become autocratic, unjust, and vaunt themselves against the God of heaven?

9. How does Daniel's assessment of what had happened to Nebuchadnezzar for seven years apply to nations in our day as well? Are contemporary rulers expected to live by God's standards even if they are not believers? Why so?

10. Why is pride such an offensive quality in a ruler? Does God promote all rulers, or at least permit them to rule, and does he also tear the ruling power away from them for similar reasons?

Lesson 6

Trusting the Living God

Daniel 6:1–28

This chapter completes the court narratives. Here, as in chapter 3, rival contemporary colleagues of Daniel accuse him of some new charge they have cooked up to catch him in a state crime. In so doing, they have even tricked the king into foolishly signing a law against praying to anyone except the king. However, once the king has signed such a stupid order, there is no way to stop the order for an execution of Daniel for disobeying it, just as Meshach, Shadrach and Abednego were trapped. All four Hebrew exiles would be taught a lesson about how the gods of Medo-Persia could be manipulated for political gain.

Once again, because of God's providential intervention, Daniel emerged at the head of a list of three administrators who were over the 120 satraps in the Medo-Persian Empire (6:1-2). But despite the best-laid plans of mortals to thwart the plans of the God of the universe, once again these opponents were foiled, and their plan backfired.

This passage has four scenes: (1) jealousy in the new government leadership (6:1–5); (2) a governmental conspiracy to get rid of foreign influence in the empire (vv. 6–12); (3) judgment carried out against Daniel (vv. 13–18); and (4) God's deliverance of Daniel (vv. 19–28). The setting of this narrative is the time when the Medo-Persian Empire ruled a good stretch of the Near East plus some adjacent areas. Our chapter ends with a doxology published as an edict by Darius (vv. 25–27), with an emphasis on "the Living God." Even during "dislocation" caused by the Babylonian exile, God was still demonstrating his power to sustain and even prosper those in the Jewish nation whom the exile had affected.

He Teaches Us How to Live – 6:1–5
Within Pagan Cultures

Unfortunately, some have tried to connect the narrative of Daniel in the lion's den with the later intertestamental story of Bel and the Dragon, which sometimes appears as one of the apocryphal additions to Daniel 14. However, not only is this story a later addition, and not in the established books of the Bible, but it is an easily seen as a polemic against idolatry and not one of the court narratives. Many judge that this later addition was borrowed from the standard story and now appears to be more contrived, especially the part that has Habakkuk transported back to Babylon to feed Daniel in the lion's den!

Daniel was made one of the "presidents" (Aramaic *sarak*) because of the way he had "distinguished himself among the administrators and the satraps" (v. 3). At this point, Daniel had more than 60 years of public service to his credit in the former Babylonian empire as he was now entering the new Medo-Persian civil service. This puts him around 80 years of age. The excellence with which he carried out his office in the government was part of his testimony for his lengthy career at that post, though the same is not true for all who are believers today and who carry on their work of employment in the various occupations. Excellence on the job is part of the witness to the Living God, even if that job is in a secular type of work.

The Darius spoken of in v. 6 may be the same person called Cyrus the Great, or his son Cambyses, who served under Cyrus as a ruler in Babylon. Or was this Darius the one also named Gubaru, whom Whitcomb surmised was appointed by Cyrus as governor of the Babylonian territories? I think Darius is the same person as Cyrus, for there are similar examples of such a dual-name phenomenon, as when the Assyrian king "Pul" is also known as "Tiglath-Pileser" (1 Chron. 5:26). This is one of the hardest problems in the book of Daniel, as we have not yet had independent archaeological evidence or confirmation.

Others are concerned because the number of administrative districts varies according to the time period. Sometimes it is 120 (Dan. 6:1); at other times it's 127 (Est. 1:1); in Persian documents it is either 20 or 27. But the word "satrap" in Aramaic referred to the "protector of the kingdom," which could also refer to smaller divisions within larger territorial units. Again, we are uncertain which it is.

Compounding the problem is that Aramaic or Greek documents from this same period have no knowledge of three "administrators," or of Daniel being part of this government. None have turned up so far, though this does not mean they do not exist; this is an argument from silence, for which the best response is silence. Herodotus (Book III, Ch. 89) claimed Darius I divided his empire into 20 provinces. But these were sub-divided into 120 smaller groups.

Daniel is depicted as a friend of Darius; thus, he is not regarded as poorly as he has been represented under Belshazzar. Just how Daniel came to the attention of Darius, we are not told. Could it be that stories of his deciphering the handwriting on the wall and his ability to interpret Nebuchadnezzar's dreams had reached the ears of the new regime? Or were his character traits well-known?

The latter seems the case, for the text specifically says Darius was attracted to Daniel for his "exceptional qualities" (v. 3) and because "he was trustworthy and neither corrupt nor negligent" (v. 4). That is quite a commendation. In such a huge operation as the empire Darius controlled, there must have always been the temptation for all sorts of lapses in morals, ethics and justice, self-enrichment plots and cover-ups.

To work with so many people as Daniel had over the years, in two different governments and in so many areas, and yet come up as "Mr. Clean" is remarkable to say the least. Surely such a record was a problem for the ambitious, envious aspirants for the office Daniel held. They must have waited daily to catch Daniel in some infraction of the rules, but none came in Daniel's day.

The administrators and satraps tried to find fault with Daniel but could not; he kept God's law and prayed daily. Had Daniel acted as did those who sought to catch him in some fault, he would have blended into the culture and accommodated the point of view of the satraps and administrators far more readily. But finding fault with Daniel, a man who kept God's word and law, would be a challenging task—unless they invented a new law. Contrary to their habit of life, it was God's laws and decrees that taught Daniel how to live. That principle is still in force even today; the Hebrew word *Torah*, "law," meant more directly "to point" or "to direct" a person as to how they should live.

Moreover, the king must have provoked the jealousy of Daniel's colleagues when he promoted him to a place of supremacy in the kingdom (v. 3). Daniel's promotion came because of his impeccable character and obvious abilities in managing governmental affairs. Thus, the conspirators shifted from his professional conduct to attacking his religious practice—their only move to entrap him.

With Patient Endurance

Daniel, keen as he was on what usually goes on in the halls of government based on years of experience, surmised there was envy and jealousy from his fellow workers in government. He must have known they were out to get him. But he would not compromise and accede to their lifestyle. That point had been demonstrated in the first court narrative in Daniel 1. There comes a point where the one faithful to the Word of God must draw a line in the sand somewhere. The Scriptures drew that line for him in the law of God.

As Solomon taught in Proverbs 27:4, "Anger is cruel and fury overwhelming, but who can stand before jealousy?" When jealousy and envy are the driving forces, absolute mischief lies in front of the servant of the Lord unless he intervenes. But the Living God, who was guiding Daniel, was greater than all the forces set to destroy him and his reputation!

He Is With Us When We Pray – 6:6–12

A Governmental Conspiracy

Conspiracies or collusions in government (or any line of work) are not a new thing, but King Darius' gullibility to it happening on his watch was amazing. Could he not see through the great and false concern of his own officials? They came as a "group" (v. 6) and greeted Darius royally. The word picture rendered here is that they conspired to "agitate," or literally "swarmed," him, even to the point of stampeding him into acting favorably to heighten his honor and reputation as a sovereign for the next thirty days (v. 7). Why only thirty days? What was so magical about thirty? These and other questions should have alerted the naïve king that more was afoot than it seemed; he was about to be taken for a fool by his own officials. They were buttering him up for some surprising event!

The proposed edict claimed to express the will of "all" his subordinate officers. Parents learn early on to disregard their children's exaggerated claims such as "Everyone dresses this way!" or "All the other parents give their kids lots of money!" Likewise, could not this monarch see he was being set up for a trap and being used to get at someone they wished to see displaced? They wanted a decree that stated: "Anyone who prays to any god or man during the next thirty days, except to you, O king, shall be thrown in the lions' den" (v. 7c). How innocent these officials pretended to be, and how suddenly they were so concerned about the king's reputation! Not one of these power-hungry thieves could be trusted, for they led the king into their trap by feigning zealously to be for his honor! And the king took the bait.

Previously, the three Hebrew captives had been the victims of tattletale "whistleblowers" by the same or similar envious colleagues in Daniel 3, but now these royal conspirators wanted an execution of any offender tossed to the lions. Should not that demand have been enough for a wise king to say: "Why so harsh a judgment, especially for first-time offenders?" Their flattery—that he should be prayed to like a god—clouded his judgment. Their apple-polishing worked! So why was this decree enacted only for thirty days, especially as it could "not be repealed" (v. 8c)? Isn't that a contradiction in terms—irrevocable act for thirty days? This was a straightforward appeal to the king's pride—and he took the whole load of foolishness, not asking what motivated these officials to argue for the fact that only the king was to be worshiped or prayed to—and for just thirty days!

Some object that there is no external evidence for the irrevocability of Medo-Persian law. But Diodorus Siculus, a second century B.C.E. historian, related how Darius III, in a fit of rage, condemned a certain Charidemus to death. Later, "When the king's anger had abated, he at once repented … but it was not possible [to retract what he had decreed], for what was done by royal authority [could not] be undone." So, the law of the Medes and the Persians was certainly irrevocable.

To make sure the king did not have time to reflect on what he was doing, these conspirators urged the king to put this decree into effect immediately (vv. 8–9). The gullible Darius obliged and enacted the edict at once. No doubt they all came with the decree already in hand for the king to affix his signature to what they had composed—such obliging supporters of the king! But notice to what lengths vanity can drive a person. The king also missed several clear signals along the way, but he must have been exceedingly hungry for praise.

An Appeal to the Government of Heaven

When Daniel learned of this edict, he took the matter directly to his heavenly Father. He went to "his upstairs room where the windows opened toward Jerusalem" (v. 10). In so doing, he carried out the teaching Solomon had given when he dedicated the temple (1 Kgs. 8:35, 38, 44, 48). He had prayed: "If [in the land of their captivity] they turn back to you with all their heart and soul … and pray to you toward the land you gave their fathers, toward the city you have chosen and the temple I have built for your [God's] name, then from heaven, your dwelling place, hear their prayer and their plea and uphold their cause" (1 Kgs. 8:48–49). In a similar manner, the prophet Jonah prayed in his hour of desperation inside the belly of that great fish as he "looked toward [God's] holy temple" (Jon. 2:4). That is how, on another occasion, David prayed as well (Pss. 5:7, 28:2).

Also, the custom of praying three times a day likewise stemmed from the psalmist who prayed to God, saying: "Evening, morning and noon, I cry in my distress, and he hears my voice" (Ps. 55:17). Moreover, when Daniel prayed, despite the jam he was in, he still was "giving thanks to his God, just as he had done before" (v. 10d). Later, the Apostle Paul would formalize this truth into a principle: "In everything by prayer and supplication with thanksgiving, let your requests be known unto God" (Phil. 4:6). Since he now acts as he "had done before," the point is that good prayer habits give deep confidence in God's providential care. Thus, the psalmist taught: "Surely [one] will never be shaken. … He will never fear shocking news; his heart is steadfast, trusting in the LORD. His heart is secure, he will have no fear; in the end he will look in triumph on his foes" (Ps. 112:6–8).

Daniel prayed with (1) *faith*, "because he had trusted in his God" (v. 23), (2) *worship* toward the city and temple God had chosen, (3) *humility*, for he knelt down on his knees before God, (4) *regularity*, for he prayed three times a day (v. 13) and (5) *thanksgiving* (v. 10d).

He Is With Us When All Is Lost – 6:13–18

The Charge by the Conspirators

There is a trace of anti-Semitism as the officials charged, "one of the exiles from Judah" (v. 13a), not "one of the presidents" or any other title for Daniel. They just charged that he "pays no attention to you, O King." They could charge such only because of the decree they had devilishly crafted—to trap Daniel! (Talk about invasion of privacy! How did these officials happen to know what Daniel's practice was other than by spying on him?) Despite the risk, he remained true to God, for there was no other place to rest one's trust and hope.

The Measures to Prevent Human Rescue

When Darius heard this, suddenly he put it all together (v. 14a). He was "deeply distressed" and "made every effort until sundown to save [Daniel]" (v. 14). Darius had been trapped by his logic, pride—and by his officials! In the name of law and order, he was now party to one of the worst injustices about to be committed in the name of the law!

Note how the Evil One can operate under the guise of laws on the books just as well as under the mantle of permissiveness! He has a conservative mask he can use, as well as a revolutionary mask. How could such a loyal civil servant be hit with the charge of sedition? It was unspeakably unfair and radically unjust!

The conspirators did not let up, especially when their hideous plan was so close to succeeding. They kept "swarming," or rallying together as a "group," around Darius, now for a third time (v. 15), reminding the king that he was bound to enforce all royal edicts. Defeated, Darius gave the order to throw Daniel to the lions, adding, "May your God, whom you serve continually, rescue you!" (v. 16) There was such jealousy and animosity from these conspirators that they wanted to ensure that the king would not stall. (Daniel may well have been the one who once saved their necks when *they* played for more time in interpreting Nebuchadnezzar's dream; see Dan. 2).

Not trusting the king's integrity, these men had him seal the lions' den— "with his own signet ring and with the rings of his nobles" (v. 17). They did not want him concocting a surprise deliverance. So distressed was Darius that he could not eat or sleep, and he went that night without any "entertainment" or his usual "diversion" (v. 18).

He Delivers Us When We Think It Least Likely – 6:18–28

A Dependence on God

So distraught was Darius after a sleepless night, that "at the first light of dawn" (1v. 9a), he rushed out to the lion's den and called in an anguished voice, "Daniel, servant of the Living God, has your God, whom you serve continually, been able to rescue you from the lions?" (v. 20). This epithet for the "Living God" is used fifteen times in the Old Testament and fourteen in the New Testament. Therefore, the teaching about the "Living God" means our God is not just a doctrine, a philosophy, an idea or "the Force;" he is alive, active, powerful, and awesome in his ability to know what is going on in the earth and to bring judgment or blessing as the occasion deserves (vv. 20, 26).

A Deliverance From God

Daniel's life had been spared by God's shutting up the mouths of the lions, for even the brute creation served as a sign to this monarch that everything on earth was under the Sovereign control of the Living God. Even the dumb animals sensed God's purpose and will, while some of God's more-intelligent beings showed a much-less-acute awareness! Some would make the stone that sealed the lion's den, upon which the king and officials' seals were placed, a type of the stone that closed the tomb of Jesus. It is said then that the story here foreshadows or predicts Jesus' own resurrection. But there is nothing here that would lead a Bible reader to make that association! Jesus' resurrection is true on other biblical and historical grounds.

Who this "angel" was is never defined in the text. But a good guess is that this may well have been none other than "the Angel of the Lord," i.e., the Lord himself, rather than one of his angelic hosts. In fact, the Greek Septuagint understood this to be a Christophany.

The King's Decree and Doxology

There is no question that the king was overjoyed at the outcome of this ordeal. He thus ordered "the men who had falsely accused Daniel" brought to the lions' den along with their wives and children" to face the punishment they had intended for Daniel (v. 24). Some are horrified by this expression of corporate solidarity, if not offended by the whole deal. But it is important to note that the Bible merely records this event without approving or disapproving of the king's command.

This event, however, does appear as an example of one of the persons of faith in Hebrews 11:33–34. Thus, the text emphasizes the positive aspects of faith without commenting on the judgment meted out by the mortal king.

Just as Nebuchadnezzar wrote to all his subjects after his seven years of being "put out to pasture," so Darius wrote to all the nations. Based on what he had experienced, he decreed: "In every part of my kingdom, people must fear and reverence the God of Daniel, for he is the Living God, and he endures forever; his kingdom will not be destroyed, his dominion will never end. He rescues and he saves; he performs signs and wonders in the heavens and on the earth. He has rescued Daniel from the power of the lions" (vv. 25–27). This doxological hymn glorifies the One and Only True God as alive and powerful.

This praise is one huge tribute from a pagan king to the Living God! Darius exalted the eternality of God and the indestructibility of his kingdom, much as Nebuchadnezzar had done in 4:3. Interestingly enough, this rescinded the "irrevocability" of the prior edict, for the king publicized his reversal of what he himself had struggled with as being what he thought irreversible. But Darius was certain that Daniel's God was the "Living God," a title he now repeated (vv. 20, 26).

Did this mean either or both kings were converted? There is just not enough data here to determine the answer to that question.

The chapter ends on a strange note as it connects the name and reign of Darius with that of Cyrus (v. 28). The writer, it seems, wants us to know the two names belong to the same person.

Conclusions

1. Envy may be one of the meanest of all human sins.
2. Envy destroys homes, churches, government, and people. It is a strong killer.
3. The Bible teaches that "the Angel of the LORD encamps around those who fear him" (Ps. 34:7).
4. It is a losing battle to fight against the people of God.
5. Be careful of the trap of personal vanity and the lengths it might drive you to.

Questions for Discussion or Reflection

1. If the satraps were made accountable to three administrators over them, with Daniel being one of three (v. 2), would this be a good enough reason to try to get the "goods" on Daniel, who served as Mr. Clean? What do you think made them uncomfortable about the way he carried out his business in that role?
2. How dangerous is it for a leader in the government to want only to hear positive reports and expressions of praise for his work? Is this true for all leaders?
3. On what basis did Daniel choose to pray toward Jerusalem three times a day? What type of admonishment does Daniel's practice bring to our prayer lives?
4. How did the king get trapped into hastily signing a decree that prayer should be made to him alone for thirty days? Was that time odd just on the face of it alone?
5. Twice the king used the phrase "the Living God." How did the events of this chapter prove that name was true for Daniel?
6. What other tasks does God assign to his good angels besides shutting the mouths of lions?
7. Was the tragic death of these jealous leaders fair and just? How can you reconcile your conclusion with high praise given to God in vv. 26–27?

Receiving and Possessing God's Eternal Kingdom

Daniel 7:1–28

Whereas the first six chapters of the book of Daniel are historical, Daniel 7–12 is predictive with a minimum of history. 7–12 has four separate visions given to Daniel at four separate times. The seventh chapter is the most comprehensive vision of the four.

From a human perspective, the Babylonian captivity of Israel had shown God was finished with the nations Israel and Judah. But God said just the opposite to the prophet Jeremiah (33:24–26):

> Have you [Jeremiah] noticed what these people are saying, "The LORD has rejected the two kingdoms he chose?" So, they despise my people and no longer regard them as a nation. This is what the LORD says, "If I have not established my covenant with day and night and the fixed laws of heaven and earth, then I will reject the descendants of Jacob and David my servant and will not chose one of his sons to rule over the descendants of Abraham, Isaac, and Jacob. For I will restore their fortunes and have compassion on them.

The vision of this seventh chapter will end any ideas that God was finished with his people at the time of the Babylonian captivity. This chapter may be the single most important one in Daniel.

This chapter also begins the "apocalyptic" section of the book as well. The narratives of Daniel's experiences end just as they began in chapter 2. In chapter 7, however, four beasts arise out of the sea, whereas in the second chapter there are four parts of the body of the colossus, thus completing the chiastic arrangement of these Aramaic chapters as noted earlier. Also, whereas the previous narratives were like third person "reports," these now move to a sort of first-person "diary" style.

There are four main interpretive approaches to understanding the times indicated by this visionary literature. The *Preterist* approach claims that all the events described in these visions are parts of past events in Israel's life. The *Futurist* interpretation sees these visions as depictions of things to come. The *historicist* approach argues that these visions trace the ideological or theological development of an age or era, such as that of Israel or the Church. And the *Idealist* approach views these visions as symbolic representations of the age-long conflict between good and evil. I take the *Futurist* point of view for these chapters because the writer places the events described here belong to what he claims are "the last days," or "the day of the Lord."

Chapter 7 takes us back to the first year of Belshazzar, around 553, some nine years after Nebuchadnezzar's death. It is the first recorded vision the prophet Daniel received. The literary form, then, is one of a dream report, which included a symbolic account of real events. But the representational or symbolic forms used in this vision do not detract from the fact that this dream is likewise a direct divine revelation to Daniel. The beasts in it are used to equate empires and kingdoms more in their internal character and inner workings, yet these visions also parallel Nebuchadnezzar's vision in chapter 2. There is little benefit in trying to detect the original source from which these symbols may have been taken, such as from myths of the ancient Near East, for there is a claim that they come directly from God.

Some think the imagery of these visions is not in use in Israel. For example, a lion with eagle's wings, or a four-headed, four-winged leopard, was not unusual for the art of that day in the ancient Near East; often the entrances to the king's palaces depicted winged beasts with a man's head. The University of Chicago Oriental Museum has a

40-ton stone sculpture of an Assyrian king, depicted as a massive "human-headed winged bull." So let us see what Daniel 7 must teach.

An Animal Vision of the Tyrants of the Past Empires – 7:1–8

Introduction

Daniel shares the first vision a dream that came to him while he was lying on his bed in the first year of the reign of Belshazzar (v. 1). Indeed, many evangelical scholars have viewed this vision as one of the key prophecies of the Bible in which God has outlined the future of the world, from the rule of the Babylonians all the way up to the Second Advent of Messiah. This would explain why this chapter is so highly regarded by many interpreters and given such importance.

Daniel saw "the four winds of heaven churning up the great sea" (v. 2). These winds were stirring up either the Mediterranean Sea or, better still, the sea of humanity (cf. Luke 21:25; Matt. 13:47; Rev. 13:1). The collocation of these four winds with a churned-up sea, together with the imagery of the animals, suggested something far different than an ordinary storm. Nevertheless, from out of the agitated sea came one animal after another, each representing an empire.

Babylon

The first animal of the four appeared "like a lion [with] the wings of an eagle" (v. 4). Such a motif was familiar to those who were accustomed to Babylonian art, as mentioned, and the allusions to the lion's speed and strength, and the eagle's soaring flight, were not lost on that original audience. The winged lion was well-known as a symbol of the Babylonian Empire. Just as the lion was the king of the beasts and the eagle was the most noble among the avian kingdom, Daniel 2 had earlier represented Babylon as the head of gold, the most valuable and cohesive of all the metals.

Daniel watched "until its wings were torn off and it was lifted from the ground" and "stood on two feet like a man," as a "heart of a man was given to it" (v. 4). This may refer to both the untimely end of this empire and God's rebuke of Nebuchadnezzar when he underwent seven years of living on grass, until his sanity was finally restored.

Medo-Persia

Daniel's second beast arising from the churning sea "looked like a bear," "raised on one side and it had three ribs in its mouth." It was told to rise and "'eat your fill of flesh'" (v. 5). This animal's huge size may well reflect the fact that the kingdom of Medo-Persia had an army of some two and a half million men (we know this from other sources, e.g., about the battle of Xerxes against Greece). That it was raised on one side fits not only with its predatory stance, but with the fact that Persia was more dominant than Media, its partner in this joint ruling arrangement, just as the colossus in Daniel 2 signified this same duality with the silver chest and the two arms. Daniel would later learn that all four animals represented four kingdoms (v. 17). In Daniel 8, the ram, which repeats the vision of the bear, also had two horns, again pointing to the two nations of Media and Persia—i.e., its dual nature!

The three ribs in the mouth of the bear are clearly three territories the bear has captured or conquered, but there is not always agreement on which three kingdoms they pointed to. But Gleason Archer noted that Cyrus and his son Cambyses were involved in three major campaigns: in 546 B.C.E. they triumphed over the Lydian kingdom in Asia Minor (Turkey), in 539 they defeated Babylon, and in 525 Cambyses annexed the kingdom of Egypt. These are the three ribs the text referred to here.

Greco-Macedonian

A third beast "like a leopard" arose from the storm-tossed sea. This is a literary composite: It had four wings like a bird and four heads. It too "was given authority to rule" (v. 6). Verse 6 begins with the words "after that," implying that these kingdoms were sequential. It is specifically pointed out that they rule in sequence, not all four at the same time.

The leopard represented Alexander the Great, who conquered and ruled vast territories from 334 to 322 but was succeeded by his generals after he died suddenly at a place remarkably close to what is today Afghanistan. The four generals were Lysimachus, Cassander, Seleucus and Ptolemy. Cassandra ruled over Macedonia and Greece; Lysimachus was given Thrace and Asia Minor; Seleucus was set over northern Syria and other eastern regions; and Ptolemy was installed as ruler over southern Syria, Palestine, and Egypt. Thus, the prophecy of four heads ruling in Alexander's place was correct and true.

Roman/Western

The fourth beast was the most terrifying and powerful of the four, with "large iron teeth." Daniel says, "It was different from all the former beasts, and it had ten horns" (v. 7). He adds that as he was focusing on the horns of this beast, a smaller, eleventh horn sprang up and uprooted three of the first horns (v. 8)— "horning in" on the others!

Daniel also says, "This horn had eyes like the eyes of a human being and a mouth that spoke boastfully." Futurists interpret this little horn to be none other than the antichrist. I argue that this fourth kingdom is that final kingdom that will appear toward the end of history when a ten-nation federation arises out of the ruins of a former empire, the Roman. Then the antichrist, the eleventh horn, will uproot three of the ten nations' rulers of that day.

Revelation 17:3 has the last world empire as a scarlet beast embracing a similar tenfold division. Likewise, Paul wrote to the Thessalonians that this same antichrist would also be called the "man of sin," "the "son of perdition," or "that wicked One" (2 Thess. 2:3, 8).

The Judge of the Whole Earth – 7:9–12

The Ancient of Days

As Daniel continued to receive the vision, the scene shifted from the agitated sea to a heavenly space, where the throne of God was then seen (v. 9). This could be a description of none other than "the High and lofty One, who inhabits eternity, whose name is Holy" (Isa. 57:15), the Lord God himself. The writing style also switches here from prose to a form of poetry consisting of short phrases. Daniel mentions that he saw *thrones* (plural) in the heavenly court, which has raised discussion among scholars. Since God is worshiped as One God, why are "thrones" needed? But this same text introduces "one like a son of man, who is given an everlasting kingdom (vv. 13–14); we assume he too has a throne. Often the New Testament depicts Jesus as the "Son of Man seated at the right hand of God" (Matt. 26:64; Mark 14:62). This, then, would meet the requirements of the plural thrones.

The title "Ancient of Days" denotes one old in age and reflects God's eternality. He is the Judge of everyone and everything, including empires (Ps. 9:5; 29:10; Isa. 28:6). His clothing is white, denoting his purity and truth, as does the whiteness of his hair (v. 9). Moreover, "his throne was flaming with fire, its wheels were all "ablaze" (v. 9). While fire is often associated with God's coming in judgment, it also can depict, as it does here, his majesty and authority. "A river of fire" (v. 10) came out from before him as judgment poured out against all wickedness. At the ready to do his will were myriads of angels as "the court was seated, and the books were opened." These "books," which are maintained in heaven, record the status of mortals on earth, and are mentioned elsewhere (12:1; Exod. 32:32; Isa. 65:6; Mal. 3:16; Lk. 10:20). It is from these books that God's judgment will proceed based on the earthly record of each person.

The Boastful Horn

As Daniel continues to watch, the boastful horn reappears. The fourth beast, or kingdom, is "destroyed and thrown into the blazing fire" (v. 11).

Verse 12's parenthetical remark points to the fact that all dominion and all authority, except that of God's dominion, would be dealt with by God, even though they "were allowed to live for a period of time." But judgment would come on these powers as well.

The Son of Man, Our Conquering Hero – 7:13–14

Coming From the Clouds of Heaven

The introductory formula of verse 2 is repeated here in v. 13, thus marking the beginning and the end of the section in vv. 2–14. The human-like figure is set forth as "one like the son of man" (v. 13). This simile stresses the humanity of his person. It is this very same title used of himself, with some 31 other instances in Matthew alone (e.g., 8:20, 9:6, 10:23). Jesus' humanity is deliberately set over against the "beastly" nature of the worldly dominions that had preceded his.

But this "son of man" also had the status of deity, for he came "with the clouds of heaven" (v. 13b). In fact, the earliest interpretation of this passage was Messianic, in the parables of the apocryphal Book of Enoch (37–71).

The "son of man" approached the "Ancient of Days" (v. 13), and an investiture ensued: The "son of man" was given absolute power and supreme authority that will never be destroyed or pass away (v. 14).

Given Eternal Dominion and Authority

The contrast between the kingdom given to the son of man and that which was possessed by the four earthly dominions could not be greater. Verse 14 repeats the lesson Nebuchadnezzar learned (2:20–22) that God alone is sovereign and that his Kingdom will be eternal.

The gift bestowed on the son of man is threefold: "authority, glory and sovereign power." The "dominion" is represented by his ruling authority. The "glory" points to the honor that will accompany his reception and use of that authority. Finally, the "sovereign power" refers to his Kingdom. These gifts would never pass away, for they were self-contained, non-contingent would endure for eternity.

All this is enough to make a believer want to sing, "Immortal, invisible, God only wise. In light inaccessible, hid from our eyes; Most blessed, most glorious, the Ancient of Days; Almighty, victorious, Thy great name we praise."

The Saints of the Most High – 7:15–27

The Interpretation of the Animal Vision

Despite the strong note of hope in verses 9–14, Daniel was still troubled by the vision (v. 15). Daniel had seen myriads of angels attending to the worship of God around his throne, so he "approached one of those standing there and asked him the true meaning of all this" (v. 16). Later, an interpreting angel might be the one named Gabriel (8:16; 9:21), but which angel it is here, his name is not stated.

The angel complied with the request and stated simply, "These great beasts are four kingdoms that will arise from the earth" (v. 17). But that is not how things will end; God will subdue those kingdoms and give to "the saints of the Most High" a kingdom that will never fade away or be destroyed (v. 18).

The Meaning of the "Holy Ones"

In Daniel 8:24, this same group, "the saints of the Most High," seem to be the "holy people," i.e., the Jews. But by New Testament times, it is the group of believers who share that portion of the future Kingdom of God that has already been manifested in Messiah's first advent (Col. 1:13). But nothing of the Church had yet been revealed to Daniel, so for him, these "holy ones" were the chosen people of Israel who believed. Scholars rightly refer to this phenomenon in interpretation as "inaugurated eschatology," or a word about the future in which there are both "now" and a "not yet" fulfillments. This dual aspect of the same single sense or meaning is illustrated in 1 John 3:2, where he teaches, "Dear friends, *now* are we children of God, and what we will be has *not yet* been made known" (emphasis mine). Thus, this group includes both those Jews who believe in Messiah in Daniel's day, and all who subsequently trust Messiah as Savior.

The Meaning of the Fourth Beast

Daniel is most concerned, however, about this fourth beast, which was so different from the other three kingdoms. Once again, what was recounted in vv. 7–8 is repeated in vv. 19–20. This beast is linked with the legs and toes of Nebuchadnezzar's colossus in Daniel 2. The vision continued to play out in Daniel's mind, with the little horn more imposing than the other horns and speaking boastfully. This eleventh horn made war with the saints and was defeating them until the Ancient of Days stepped in and rendered a "judgment in favor of the holy people of the Most High" (vv. 21–22).

The interpreting angel finally explained the fourth beast: It would appear on earth following the rise and demise of the preceding three kingdoms. Also, "it will be different from all the other kingdoms and will devour the whole earth" (v. 23c–d). So different is it that it cannot be likened to any animal, as the other kingdoms were. It just trampled everything in its way, in wanton destruction (v. 23e).

The angel also explains, "The ten horns are ten kings who will come from this kingdom," but this little horn, or new king, will subdue three of the ten kings (v. 24). "Another king will arise and be marked by four characteristics: (1) he will blaspheme the Most High God, (2) he will oppress the saints of the Most High, trying to wear them down, (3) he will attempt to change the set times (perhaps by implementing a new calendar of religious festivals?), and (4) he will use his power to oppress the saints for "a time, times and a half time" [literally, "a dividing"] (v. 25). This last phrase means three and a half years, for a "time" means a "year" (cf. 8:14). It is repeated later in Daniel and in Revelation (Dan. 12:7; Rev. 12:14). This period will be between the desecration of the Temple and the end of history. The reign of this evil king ends as quickly as it begins, for "he will be stripped of his power and completely destroyed forever" (v. 26). This is mandated by the "court," which again recalls the throne scene in vv. 9–11. Instead of this fourth kingdom, with a ten-horned confederacy governed by the same one named in Revelation 13 and 17, God's Kingdom will take its place forever, and all rulers will worship and serve God (v. 27).

The Aftermath

This seventh chapter concludes much like Ecclesiastes 12:13, "Now hear the conclusion to the whole matter." But if the matter is resolved, or so this would seem to imply, why is Daniel still "deeply troubled" by his thoughts and his "face turned pale" (v. 28)? Surely, he understood the basic plan of God announced here, but was the issue that he wished to know more details? He will indeed learn more in what follows, for his prophecy has not ended at this point. Daniel wants readers to expect more to come to clarify some of the matters.

Conclusions

1. Every government on earth can only act under the permission or direct will of God. He, the Living God, is sovereign over everything. None of the forms of human government will survive the final destruction of the antichrist and all those who carry out his will; they will all be vanquished forever.

2. God has a plan and a timetable for the events that are happening now and for the end of the whole, but the dates are known only to him and to no one else.

3. Suffering is not to be judged an unexpected event in the life of a Saint and glory and for our growth in Messiah.

Questions for Discussion or Reflection

1. What makes this fourth empire so awesome to Daniel and to us? Is the USA in your judgment included in this fourth empire?

2. What other passages in Scripture speak of this "little horn" or about the "antichrist"? What are the characteristics of this person?

3. Who is the one who comes with the clouds of heaven and how does his appearance fit the sequence of events in the rest of the Scriptures?

4. Who is the "Ancient of Days" and what actions are given to him to accomplish?

5. Who are the "holy ones," the "people of the Saints" of "the Most High"?

Lesson 8

Understanding the Ironies of History

Daniel 8:1–27

The Aramaic section began in 2:4b—with a prediction of about four world empires that would precede God's final Kingdom—and ends at 7:28 by presenting in that chapter the same empires that will expire before a fifth kingdom from heaven would be set up that would last for all eternity. Daniel now writes in Hebrew for the rest of his book, and chapter 8 begins by tracing and expanding on two of the animals, now pictured in domestic forms, but taken from the previous four animals, namely the second and third kingdoms in chapter 7.

His vision shifts from Babylon, where the previous visions had been given. He now sees himself in the citadel (Hebrew *birah*) of Susa (8:2). But this was "in the third year of King Belshazzar's reign" (v. 1), so it came to him before the events of chapter 5. Susa, the ancient capital of Elam, was set to become one of prominent cities in the Persian Empire. This "vision" (vv. 1, 2, 13, 15, 26) was granted to him around 550, when Cyrus broke away from Astyages the Mede and established the joint kingdom of Medo-Persia. Also note the repeated rhetorical feature of the "I, Daniel" formula that occurs at the start and end of the vision (vv. 2, 27) and at the beginning of its interpretation (v. 15).

Between Two World Empires – Medo-Persia and Greece – 8:1–8

The Place of the Vision

Daniel, now about 69 years, was transported in the spirit to the citadel of Susa (also called Shushan), or more precisely, just outside the city "beside the Ulai Canal" (v. 2). This city was some 230 miles east of Babylon and 120 miles north of the Persian Gulf. The Ulai Canal was an artificial one, which widened at points to some 900 feet wide and is the same as the classical Eulaeus. However, it was large enough for Alexander the Great to sail his fleet down the Abi-diz, the waterway on the east side of the city. Later this was made a royal city by Cyrus (Neh. 1:1; Est. 1:2), but here it is called a "citadel" or "fortress." It was in this city where the Code of Hammurabi was later discovered. The later palace built by Darius was located here, as was Queen Esther's.

The word used for "vision" is the same as the Hebrew word for a "revelation," *hazon.* Such a "revelation" came for God himself, and not from a human being or from any secondary sources.

The Ram and the He-Goat

Daniel was first shown a two-horned ram "standing by the canal." He writes, "One of the horns was longer than the other but grew up later" (v. 3). As he watched the ram charge toward the west, then to the north and finally southward. "No animal could stand up against it, and none could rescue from its power" (v. 4). It did just what it jolly well pleased and proceeded to become great in influence.

Meanwhile, a male goat appeared "with a prominent horn between its eyes" (v. 5a). This unicorn-like animal came from the west. It "crossed the whole earth without touching the ground," so swift were its movements (v. 5b–c). With such speed and force, this buck goat shattered the ram's two horns. The ram hardly knew what hit it and was powerless to stand up against this one-horned goat. Thus, the ram was trampled to the ground, and "none could rescue the ram from its power" (v. 7b–c). So, the goat became exceedingly great. But at the peak of its power, "the power of the large horn was broken off" and replaced by four horns that "grew up toward the four winds of heaven" (v. 8).

Between Two World Leaders – 8:9–14

A Horn Out of the Four Horns

Verse 20 specifically says the "two-horned ram … represents the kings of Media and Persia." It will go on to say that "the shaggy goat is the king of Greece, and the large horn between his eyes is the first king" (v. 21). So, the goat was none other than Alexander the Great.

With an army of 120,000, Alexander had crossed India to the Indus River, but at the Ganges, his warriors were fed up with his campaigning and refused to continue. Thus, India would not experience the infusion of Greek culture because of conquest. However, in twelve years, Alexander had conquered most of the known world. He died from excessive drinking, and his kingdom was subsequently divided into four parts for his four generals: Seleuces, Ptolemaeus, Cassander, and Lysimachus. Cassandra received Macedonia and Greece, Lysimachus got Thrace and much of Asia Minor, Seleucus received Assyria and a huge amount of territory to the east and Ptolemy received Egypt and part of Palestine.

From one of these four generals "another horn" sprang up (v. 9a). While this horn begins small, it quickly grew in power and moved southward, eastward and toward the "Beautiful land" (vv. 9–10). That label of being "Beautiful" is also used by the prophet Ezekiel for the land of Israel (Ezek. 20:6, 15). This little horn continued to grow until it reached "the host of the heavens, and it threw some of the starry host down to earth and trampled on them" (v. 10). In so doing, it is claiming equality with God. This horn must represent Antiochus IV Epiphanes (the latter word meaning "God manifest"), especially his conflict with the Jewish people.

This little horn exalted itself as if it were the "Prince of the host" (v. 11a), an allusion to the Lord as "LORD of hosts." It went on to "take away the daily sacrifice" in Jerusalem, which should have been offered to the Lord, and overthrew the place of his sanctuary (v. 11).

That was a mistake—an attack on God's sacrifice was an attack on God himself. Thus, Antiochus stole for himself the daily sacrifice from the temple. A description of what happened is recorded in the deuterocanonical book of 1 Maccabees 1:21–49. Antiochus entered the temple of God and took away the seven-branched golden menorah and the temple vessels, as he forbade any more daily sacrifices to be offered in the temple to God. Instead, he ordered the Jews should profane the Sabbaths and the festival days, leave their children uncircumcised, and worship at idol sites with swine's flesh.

Verse 12 is very tough to translate, as the grammar and allusions are hard to establish, but this "little horn" gained military support against the offering of the daily sacrifice to God as the transgressions of the people mounted up. Consequently, "truth was cast down to the ground" and error was given free reign for the moment.

Daniel heard a holy one speaking to another: "How long will it take for the vision to be fulfilled?" (v. 13) This same question occurs fairly frequently in the Psalms and prophets as well (Ps. 6:3; Isa. 6:11; Zech. 1:12). The thought behind the question is that God always will limit evil's rule and reign. The evil referenced in v. 13 refers to what happened in vv. 9–12.

Antiochus IV represented the "now" aspect of evil in the second century B.C.E. that a "not yet" antichrist would repeat in the last days, only it would be more severe. In the last days before Messiah's return, the antichrist's evils will be not unlike those of Antiochus Epiphanes earlier in history. This is because the language moves beyond Antiochus IV; that is, the antichrist will come when the rebels have become completely wicked (v. 23a; cf. 2 Thess. 2:3). Antichrist's self-magnification will exceed all bounds (23; cf. 2 Thess. 2:3–5). Both Antiochus and the future antichrist will cause astounding devastation and will, for the moment, succeed in whatever they do (vv. 23-24).

The answer to the holy one's "how long?" (v. 13) was 2300 morning and evening sacrifices (v. 14), or 1150 days (by halving this number, as two sacrifices were offered on the same day). That is three years and two months. The historian Josephus said that was the exact amount of time the temple service was interrupted by Antiochus IV Epiphanes (cf. 1 Macc. 4:36–61). This was the amount of time that elapsed between the desecration of the Lord's altar by Antiochus and its re-consecration by Judas Maccabeus on Kislev (our December) 25, 165 B.C.E.

Likewise, the Antichrist will rage in the future, just as Antiochus did in his day, only in the future it will be for three and a half years, i.e., the second half of the seven final years of Daniel's 70th week (9:24–27).

Once again, one of these four new horns sprouted "another horn" (v. 9a), not to be confused with "another horn" that arose out of the ten horns of the fourth kingdom. Instead, this is a ruler who gained control of one of the four horns that came out of the third world kingdom, which was from Alexander the Great's empire. Yet even after this horn's most-humble beginnings, it grew in power toward the south and toward the "Beautiful Land," which points more definitely to Israel.

Between the "Now" of History and the "Not Yet" of the Future – 8:15–27

Two Appearances

Whether Daniel awoke and was briefly conscious to reflect on what he had seen thus far or not is not certain, but he was soon back to a visionary state. There he saw a man-like (Hebrew *geber*, a "strong man," a macho type of male) figure. This man spoke from the Ulai River; but who was he? It might have been an angel, such as Gabriel (also meaning "man of God") or Michael, the only other angel named in the Bible. The one who looked like a man, however, spoke with the voice of a man as he ordered, "Gabriel tell this man the meaning of this vision" (v. 16).

A commanding voice to Gabriel, one would think, would have to be from God himself. The angel Gabriel appears only here, in 9:21, and later in the message delivered to Mary (Luke 1:19, 26). Later, the angel named Michael will appear in Daniel 10:13, 21; 12:1.

The "Time of the End"

As Gabriel came near to where Daniel stood, Daniel became terrified and fell into a "deep sleep" with his face to the ground (v. 17). However, the angel "touched him" and raised him to his feet (v. 18). Nevertheless, Daniel's reaction was very much like the Apostle John's reaction on the Isle of Patmos when he too was approached by an angel (Rev. 22:8). But what affected him was not the medium but the message, for the words also concerned "the time of the end" (v. 17d).

Daniel was then told "happen in the time of wrath" (v. 19a). Does this interpretation answer the question in v. 13, "How long will it take for the vision to be fulfilled?" or is there both a near and a distant combined meaning here as well? Surely it means God's wrath on Israel at the time of Antiochus IV Epiphanes; that is why v. 19 repeats the vision is about what will happen "in the time of wrath." That is also why some interpreters justifiably see it as God's future time of judgment and as a type of the Antichrist, who would come before Messiah's return.

So, the whole chapter is partially fulfilled historically in the decrees and actions of Antiochus IV Epiphanes, but he would foreshadow a future world leader, who, would likewise rule to the disadvantage of the Jewish people in the end-times.

Gabriel makes clear that the two-horned ram represented the kings of Media and Persia (v. 20). Goldingay, in his commentary on Daniel, notes that the ram was a natural representation for Persia, for in the zodiac Persia was under Aries, the ram. Gabriel also identified the "shaggy goat" as the "king of Greece" with "the large horn between his eyes" as the "first king" (v. 21). While Alexander was not the "first king," he was certainly the greatest, and none other than "the large horn between the goat's eyes" (v. 21). Moreover, the four horns that replaced the "large horn" that was broken off would be the four generals who would divide up the empire and assume Alexander's place after his death.

The Stern-Faced King

Toward the close of the reigns of these generals, when the rebels had excelled in wickedness (v. 23a), a "stern-faced king" would arise. This would be Antiochus IV Epiphanes (who would later rule from 175–164). In 169 B.C.E. he invaded Egypt and was highly successful at first (see Dan. 11:25–30; also 1 Macc. 1:16–20 and 2 Macc. 5:1–14).

Antiochus' absence from Jerusalem gave an opportunity for those in Jerusalem, who resented his interference with the High Priestly office as this stern-faced king would place his own appointee as High Priest—who turned out to be Menelaus. Antiochus' surprise return to Jerusalem caught the insurgents off-guard and led to several reprisals, including the plunder of the temple, the installation of an altar to the god Zeus (a real abomination), and the offering of a sow in temple of God (an equally great insult and desecration).

Both Antiochus and the king who is to come are both predicted to be "stern-faced," or better translated, "defiant, shameless" or "insolent." The same word was used for the "impudent looks" of a harlot in Proverbs 7:13. They also will be "master[s] of intrigue" (v. 23b), cause "astonishing desolation" and "succeed in whatever" they do (v. 24). Accordingly, the two of them will have a propensity for double-dealing and being cunningly adroit. As supermen, they will be admired by the entire world, but their power will not come from themselves but from the energy Satan himself will give to them (2

Thess. 2:9). But his most despicable feature will be that both acted as persecutors and destroyers of the Holy people, i.e., Israel (v. 24).

Antiochus was destroyed, "but not by his own power" (v. 24). If that is the correct rendering, then 1 Maccabees 6:8–13 explained that Antiochus was not slain in battle, but he received word in Babylon that the Maccabees had defeated his army and won control over Israel once more. At that, he fell sick and called his friends to tell them he was going to die. He explained, according to this record, "I remember the evils that I did at Jerusalem ... therefore for this cause I perish."

Daniel was told to "seal up the vision" (v. 26)—not because it was incomprehensible or contained some hidden code, but because it was sure to take place and because its word should be preserved against the day of its fulfillment.

This vision left Daniel "exhausted ... and ill for many days" (v. 27). These visions he saw and what he had explained to him were clear, but how could that all take place when the world had never seen a Medo-Persian or a Greek empire, never mind all the detail about a stern-faced king of the future and the like? But *history* is the final interpreter of prophecy, as Jesus reminds us in John 13:19, and it finally points to the fact that God, not these nations, is the One in control.

Conclusions

1. While we are given more detail on the second and third empires mentioned in Daniel 2 and 7, the identities of the second and third empires are set forth in detail so that we might praise God for the dependability and truthfulness of his Word.

2. God is still sovereign over mortals and nations, for the plan of history is not theirs but his.

3. If God gave this prophetic word so clearly in the 6th century B.C.E. that most all agree with its meaning, which was fulfilled from the sixth to the second century, why are critical scholars so slow to acknowledge Scripture's prophetic nature and truthfulness?

Lesson 9

Praying God's Promises
and Receiving the Answers

Daniel 9:1–27

Introduction

Daniel was a man of prayer! We are told that he opened his windows toward Jerusalem thrice daily to pray (6:10). Undoubtedly, just as often he opened the books to God's Word, especially since he studied "the word of the LORD given to Jeremiah the prophet" (9:2)—a scroll containing these Scriptures that may well have been carried from his homeland of Israel by the exiles. This high regard for the Scriptures is likewise very evident when we hear Daniel praying, for he prays from a series of subtly woven quotations from what we today call the Old Testament. He must also have memorized substantial portions of the Scripture.

Previously, back in Israel there had been priests and prophets and the temple to assist the people in worship, but now they were thrown exclusively on God's Word as their only aid in worshiping him, for the temple had been destroyed and they now lived in exile. Some say this may have been one of the exile's greatest results. As usually happens in situations like these, when the people turned to the writings that came as a revelation from God, they also found that God drew nearer to them. This is because God himself had ordered that real and vital worship was most clearly linked with the study and obedience of the Scriptures.

Ronald Wallace (*Daniel*, IVP, 1979) illustrated this point by citing the case of Dr. Martin Niemöller, who, during World War II, spoke of his sense of real loss. After he languished in a prison for 18 months, the Nazis condemned him to death on March 2, 1938; with the conviction, everything was taken from him, including his Bible. He begged to have it restored, and it finally was. His own confession was that this book was the source of his strength and comfort; it was what he needed most.

In a comparable situation, Daniel pored over the books as God breathed into him new life as he saw all over again what God had done for the worthies of the past, such as Abraham, Moses, and Jeremiah. Daniel was moved by the same concerns, perplexities, and the desire for God's glory as his people had evidenced in the past; he too experienced the Babylonian exile. It was God's Word that would be the mainstay of lives.

Sincere Prayer Is Needed in Critical Times – 9:1–2

Darius the Mede

The first mention of "the first year of Darius son of Xerxes" (a Mede by descent; 9:1) acts here as both the fact that sets the scene and as a key problem in the book of Daniel. I argued earlier that "Darius the Mede" was the same man as Cyrus II, the first king of the Medo-Persian Empire after the fall of the Babylonian Empire. Critical scholars widely regard this reference to "Darius the Mede, the son of Xerxes" as a historical blunder, since Xerxes was Darius I's son, not his father. But conservative scholars have answered, as did Wiseman, that Xerxes (also called Ahasuerus) was an Achaemenid royal title, or a dynastic throne name, that was also applied to Cyrus II. Also, William Foxwell Albright argues that "Darius" may have been an old Iranian title, like the Egyptian "Pharaoh." So far this is only a theory, but it has some precedent in that other rulers in the Near East had more than one name, as was true of "Pul" (2 Kgs. 15:19, 29; 1 Chron. 5:26), also known as "Tiglath-Pileser." Whatever the solution to the identity of "Darius," Daniel was referring to the first year of the Medo-Persian Empire, 539, which Ezra 1:1 also calls "the first year of Cyrus, king of Persia." Accordingly, what Daniel may have been getting at is that the identity of Darius and Cyrus are the same! (See also my *Excursus*, which argues that King Darius is the same person as Cyaxerxes as Josephus advocated in the first century.)

The Seventy Years of Jerusalem in the Desolation

The reference to the "Scriptures" in v. 2 is literally "the scrolls" or "the books" (Hebrew *basseparim*). This word may well be a technical term by this time in the history of Israel's growing number of biblical scrolls, as a revelation from God. Even more startling is the reference to "the word of the LORD given to Jeremiah" (v. 2). Jeremiah's writings, penned less than 70 years earlier, were instantaneously classified as part of those scrolls that were so highly regarded that they called them the "word of the LORD." There was no waiting for an alleged Council at Jamnia (that later convened in 90 C.E.) to determine and vote on what was authorized and what was not part of the authentic books of the Bible. In fact, at Jamnia the rabbis only discussed the interpretation of Ecclesiastes and Song of Solomon—not which books were truly canonical and authoritative!

More particularly, Daniel learned from Jeremiah 25:11, 29:10 that the "desolation of Jerusalem would last seventy years" (Dan. 9:2). That is why Daniel "turned to the Lord God and pleaded with him in prayer and petition, in fasting and in sackcloth and ashes" (v. 3). The reason God required these seventy years would be explained in 2 Chronicles 36:21 as the amount of time needed for Jerusalem's desolation to fulfill the Sabbaths that Judah had neglected in their history. So, Daniel took God at his word. God's promises were not meant to detract us from prayer, but to teach us what it is we are to pray for.

Daniel's use of fasting during this time showed that as his body outwardly grieved, so did his soul grieve over the sad state of his people and the times they were living in (cf. Zech. 7:1–7). His mourning and use of sackcloth pointed to the fact that his penitence for himself and his people was just as sincere and real as the cries of his heart. Just because God had given a divine decree, however, did not mean God's purpose would be accomplished regardless of the prayers or actions of his people. The same God who had decreed the judgment was the same God who had raised up intercessors like a Daniel!

Fervent Prayer Calls for Confession of Our Sin and the Sin of Our Nation – 9:4–19

The Great and Awesome God – 9:4

Daniel's prayer is a mosaic of phrases taken from the biblical scrolls he had surely pored over and committed to memory. Such use of scriptural languages and sentiments to give voice to our own public prayers has a long history. The best examples of the use of Scripture in prayer are seen in our Lord Jesus (Jn. 17), or even of the prayers of Jonah while stuck in the bowels of the great fish (Jon. 2).

Daniel began with a concern for dates seen in Jeremiah's prophecy, but he soon forgot all about dates as his mind shifted to a more basic, more critical issue: The hope of Israel's return to God and their return to their land were his uppermost concerns. God is addressed as "Lord," meaning "master, overlord" (Hebrew *'Adonai*) and "the great and awesome God, who keeps covenant with all who love him" (v. 4). Moses first used the title "the great and awesome God" (Hebrew *ha'el haggadol*, Deut. 7:21) to inspire confidence in Israel, as they had awful dread of the Canaanites. Later, Nehemiah would begin his prayer the same way (Neh. 1:5). Even though Daniel is not from a priestly family and not even described as a prophet in Scripture, neither he nor we need any special permission to intercede for others, including those in our own nation. It is from the joy of making God's name great and as awesome as it is that both Daniel and we are thereby given perspective on the problems we face, just as Moses earlier taught Israel (Deut. 7:21).

Moreover, God "keeps his covenant" and gives "grace" (*hesed*) to "all those who love him and obey his commands" (v. 4, cf. Deut. 7:9; Exod. 20:5–6). Loving God and obeying him go together, as Jesus emphasized: "If you love me, you will obey what I command" (John 14:15).

Communal Confession of Our Sin – 9:5–6

Daniel's prayer of confession begins with five synonyms for sin: "sinned," "done wrong," "been wicked," "have rebelled" and "have turned away" from God's commands and laws. But Daniel also identifies with his people, using "us," "we" or "our" some 39 times in this prayer. Both he and they needed God's forgiveness, so why would he only pray for them as if he were exempt? Instead, he identified with them as he confessed the sin of the whole community. Moreover, Israel had not listened to the warnings of God's "servants, the prophets" (v. 6). The prophets had clearly warned Israel's kings, princes, fathers and all the people by speaking in the name of the Lord, but all to no profit.

The Lord Is Righteous; We Are Shamed – 9:7–8

All the time these warnings and prophetic messages were going out to all Israel, the Lord remained righteous. He had been in the right all the way in every one of his dealings with Israel. But the nation had been in the wrong. No wonder they were "covered with shame" (v. 8a). Now Israel sat in shame in countries where God had scattered them.

The Lord's Mercy Will Prevail – 9:9–10

Daniel concludes his confession with the assurance that God is merciful and "forgiving." Both words in Hebrew are plural, stressing how great is God's mercy and forgiveness. Those were the same words used when God revealed himself to be of the same nature when he forgave Israel for the golden calf (Exod. 34:5–6). Had God not taken the initiative in extending his manifold mercy and abundant forgiveness, Israel and all the world would still be deadlocked in sin and rebellion.

Theological Reflection on God's Justice – 9:11–14

As a result of Israel's sin, the sworn judgments of God set forth by Moses in Leviticus 26:14–45 and Deuteronomy 28:15–68 came into play in the experience of Israel and Judah. Daniel added that this was recorded "in the law of Moses, the servant of God" (v. 11c). It all happened "just as it is written" (v. 13a); the warnings had happened.

The reason the Lord did not hesitate to bring this disaster upon Jerusalem was because he is "righteous" (v. 14b). This section has many allusions and quotations from Deuteronomy and Jeremiah. While other cities also were destroyed in other nations, Jerusalem was in a special category; its citizens had had more warnings from God, and God himself dwelt in Jerusalem. Thus, when the city did not repent, God did not "hesitate" (Hebrew *shaqad*; "kept watch over" or "kept disaster ready," v. 14a) to bring calamity due to Israel's sin, rebellion, and disobedience.

A Transition From Confession to Supplication – 9:15–19

With the introductory word "Now," Daniel went from confession to supplication. Only now did Daniel begin to make his requests known to God. So earnestly did he pray that he appealed to God's name seven times (vv. 15, 16, 17, 19).

As God had kept his word about his judgments, he could also be trusted to keep his word about his promises. As James 4:2 says, "You do not have, because you do not ask God." Thus, the invitation, "Come near to God and he will come near to you" (Jas. 4:8). We, like

Daniel, must call if we wish God to answer us (Jer. 33:3), for then he will show us "great and unsearchable things [we did] not know."

Previously, Israel had been preserved by God's "mighty hand" (v. 15) as they came out of Egypt. In so doing, God had made a name and reputation for himself, which "endures to this day." But now in Daniel's day, Israel had made God's name an "object of scorn" (vv. 15d–16d), for as God had to bring judgment on the people because of their sin, it appeared to the pagan nations that God could not preserve his own temple from Nebuchadnezzar, much less from the Assyrian gods of Marduk and Nebo. Israel had brought reproach on the name of God.

Because Israel had tarnished God's name by their multitude of sins, including idol-worship, Daniel begged God to vindicate his own reputation and listen to the prayer of his servant (v. 17). Jerusalem, Daniel urged in prayer, was "the city that bears your Name" (v. 18b). But the place of his worship was now a "desolate sanctuary" (v. 17c). Daniel implored God to honor his word and end the present situation as he had promised through the prophet Jeremiah.

With a mosaic of familiar phrases from throughout the Old Testament, Daniel felt confident his prayer would be heard. The three glorious objects of God's past and future love would all feel his intervention: his people Israel, his city Jerusalem, and his sanctuary, his temple.

Answers to Prayer Shape History – 9:20–27

Answers to a Highly Esteemed Man – 9:2–23

Daniel never formally ended his prayer; while he was still praying, a messenger named Gabriel arrived with news that his prayer had been heard (vv. 20–21). Gabriel was the interpreting angel Daniel had seen in an earlier vision of the ram and goat (8:16). He may also have been the unidentified interpreter for Daniel when the four creatures arose from the sea (7:16).

Gabriel came in "swift flight" (v. 21b; Hebrew `wp, "to fly," may also be read as *y'p*, "to be weary, to faint," of Daniel's great weariness) about "the time of the evening sacrifice," or mid-afternoon, usually at 3 p.m. This time signal does not prove that sacrifices had been reinstituted, just that the regular time for such was still remembered. Gabriel, here seen as a man, had come to "instruct" Daniel and to give him "insight and understanding" (v. 22). He was told that an answer to his prayer was on the way, "as soon as [he] began to pray" (23a). He was also told that he was "highly esteemed" (23b, cf. 10:19), among other things, because of his humility and faith in the promises of God.

The Six Purposes of the "Seventy 'Sevens'" – 9:24

Some think that the next four verses are some of the hardest and most difficult in the Bible. One thing is for sure: Old Testament higher criticism has complicated this text far more than necessary.

Daniel is told that a unit of seventy units of seven (or seventy heptads), i.e., seventy sevens of years are decreed (i.e., "ordained," "determined") for Israel and for their holy city of Jerusalem. Recall that Daniel had begun his prayer to God about the seventy years of Captivity that Jeremiah had mentioned (Jer. 25:11–14; 29:10–14), for he assumed those seventy years had been completed.

Most conservative interpreters take "seventy sevens" to mean a period of 490 years, thus distinguishing it from the 70 years of captivity in Babylon. This 490 is then divided into three sets or units of time: (1) a seven-set of sevens amounting to 49 years, (2) a 62-set of sevens equaling 434 years, and after an interruption or unspecified time, and (3) a final one-set of seven or 7 years (vv. 25-26). More on that later, but for now we will look at the six reasons for these seventy heptads.

The first objective in v. 24 was that these seventy years were to "finish transgression." Transgression here is used as a term for sin in general, which will finally end with the glorious second coming of Messiah's eternal reign. Human rebellion will finally end when all the "seventy sets of 'seven'" are finished.

The second objective, like the first, was to "put an end to sin." God himself will restrain sin as the eternal state begins. This will come at the end of human history as God's Kingdom replaces the succession of human kingdoms.

The third purpose is "to atone for wickedness." This was provided for at the crucifixion of Messiah. So complete would be the payment and removal of wickedness that Jeremiah taught, "'In those days, at that time,' declares the LORD, 'search will be made for Israel's guilt, but there will be none, and for the sins of Judea, but none will be found among her either, for I will forgive the remnant I spare'" (Jer. 50:20).

Most commentators note that these first three purposes are negative—i.e., they deal with "transgression," "sins" and "wickedness." The last three of the six purposes or objectives speak to the positive side of things.

The fourth objective of these years is "to bring in everlasting righteousness." What better description of the wonderful nature of the coming Kingdom of God. Now that sin has been banished from God's rule and reign, a nation involved in sin (9:7, 14, 16) is not possible any longer.

The fifth purpose is "to seal up vision and prophecy" (v. 24e). This refers to closing a scroll for preservation by rolling it up and placing a seal on it. But sealing also meant to authenticate the contents by placing one's seal and signature on it, assuring that what was promised would happen exactly as written. It pointed, then, to all the predictions about the future of Israel and the third temple that was to be built in Jerusalem.

Finally, the sixth purpose was "to anoint the most holy" (v. 24f). The exact object is not stated (is it "the holy *One*," "the holy *place*," *or* "the holy *altar*"?), but the best reading is that it refers to the re-consecration God's temple as described in Ezekiel 40–44. This expression is never used of a person, so it is no reference to the Messiah or to his Church, nor is it a reference to the outpouring of the Holy Spirit; it is, therefore, best restricted to the coming temple in Jerusalem.

These six purposes speak of the final accomplishment of God's purpose for the whole historic process. Some of this began to be established with our Lord's first coming, but there remains much to be done in connection with his second advent. These six purposes just telescope the work at his first and second comings into a combined set.

The Three Sets of Seven – 9:25–27

Where do we begin counting off the years for all these "seventy 'sevens'"? The starting point, according to v. 25a, is "the decree to restore and rebuild Jerusalem." If a distinction is made between the restoration and rebuilding of the city versus rebuilding the temple, then the starting date is easy: It is Artaxerxes' decree given to Nehemiah authorizing the restoration of the rebuilding of the walls of the city of Jerusalem in 445 B.C.E. (Neh. 2:1–8); that is the only decree that mentions the rebuilding of Jerusalem. No other date seems to fit or embrace what this mandate about the city is all about. Verse 25d focuses on the city and not the temple, for Jerusalem "will be rebuilt with streets and a trench, but in times of trouble." Nehemiah did oversee the rebuilding of the walls of Jerusalem in just that short a period—fifty-two days.

What then is the endpoint for the first sixty-nine "sevens?" Gabriel told Daniel it would extend "until the Anointed One, the ruler who comes." Sir Robert Anderson, in *The Coming Prince*, tried to design an exact calendar using what he called prophetic years of 360 days each (instead of 365) starting in 445 B.C.E., to say this all ended exactly on the date of Messiah's crucifixion, which he incorrectly put in C.E. 32. This is a much-too-rigid approach with several unproven assumptions.

Everything here hangs on the identity of the "Anointed One." This refers to the Messianic King, Jesus. The *terminus ad quem* then is fixed and must fall sometime during Jesus' earthly life, preferably when he was "cut off" (v. 26b). This will happen as the first 69 sets of seven, or 483 years, expire, with only one set of seven years left!

The first set of seven heptads, then, added up to 49 years. In this period, Jerusalem would "be rebuilt with streets and a trench, but in times of trouble" (v. 25d). Nehemiah did his part on the walls in fifty-two days (Neh. 6:15). What this "trench" (Hebrew *haruts*) consists of is not stated, but it is some kind of moat around the city to increase the height and the obstacle of the walls.

The next heptad is one of sixty-two sevens, lasting 434 years. We are not told anything special about this set except that it combines with the previous seven heptads to make a total of 69 sets of seven, or 483 years. Therefore, from the decree of Artaxerxes in 445, we come to approximately 27 C.E., the probable year which year was when Messiah began his ministry and was baptized by John the Baptist.

Verse 26 noted, "*After* the sixty-two sevens, the Anointed One will be cut off and will have nothing." Thus, upon the completion of 69 sets of heptads, or 483 years, Messiah would be crucified, declared Daniel in the sixth century B.C.E. Thus, there would be a gap of undetermined length between the first Good Friday crucifixion of our Lord and the commencement of the last set of seven years. But the length of this break or gap is uncertain, for it included the death of Messiah around 30 C.E. as well as the destruction of the Jerusalem and the temple (v. 26c). Thus, the sequence of years came to a halt as indicated by the events of 30 C.E. (the crucifixion) and 70 C.E. (the Roman defeat of Jerusalem). Gabriel will not speak more on the final seventieth week until verse 27.

Once Messiah had been crucified and the second temple destroyed, "the end will come like a flood" (v. 26e). Then, who are "the people of the ruler who will come?" (v. 26b). This one will destroy the city and the sanctuary, as the Roman conqueror Titus did in 70 C.E. But there is both a "now" meaning and a "not yet" sense to this text, for that ruler who is to come turned out to be one of the Seleucids named Antiochus IV Epiphanes in 168 B.C.E. Then it will be the Roman General Titus who will come in 70 C.E., and finally in the "not yet" aspect of this prophecy, it will be the future antichrist who will demolish the third temple and attack Israel in that final day of history.

The final seven-year-set brings us to the completion of God's program. The "ruler who shall come" (v. 26c) "will confirm a covenant with many" for that last seven-year period, but in the middle of those seven years, he will "put an end to sacrifice and offering" (v. 27a–b). Thus, he will indicate his opposition to God's people. Though Antiochus had desecrated the temple by offering a hog on the altar and setting up an idol or something abominable, he did not destroy the temple or Jerusalem (1 Macc. 1:31, 38). Instead, this refers to the future antichrist, who will set up in the temple something filthy and loathsome to God and the Jewish people. Jesus warned, "When you see the abomination of desolation spoken of by the prophet Daniel … let those who are in Judea flee to the mountains" (Matt. 24:15–16). This will go on until complete destruction is poured out on the one who makes desolate.

In summary, as my teacher Dr. Robert Duncan Culver taught, five facts are included in this prophecy: (1) the 70 weeks are 490 years, which relate to the then-future of Israel. (2) These weeks are divided into three periods of time of seven, sixty-two, and one, which follow one another except for the unspecified gap time between the 69th and 70th week. (3) The first 69 weeks ran out during the lifetime of Messiah and before his crucifixion. (4) The death of Messiah (about 30 C.E.) and the destruction of Jerusalem (C.E. 70) indicate a time gap or a break between the 69th and 70th week. (5) The 70th week deals with a seven-year relationship between that future antichrist and Daniel's people Israel, wherein he breaks a covenant he has made with Israel to build a third temple, and that final seven-year period, which ends in the 1000-year reign of Messiah that comes just before the eternal state.

Conclusions

1. Even though this text may seem difficult because it is so detailed, Jesus said in Matthew 24:15, whoever reads what Daniel the prophet wrote, "let the reader understand." Jesus meant this text to be understood!

2. The death of Messiah and the fall of Jerusalem were not unknown as future events for our Lord, but they were included within his eternal plan.

3. Look how effective prayer can be, for when Daniel receives an answer to his prayer, God gives to Daniel a detailed explanation of what will happen, all the way to the end of this age!

Questions for Discussion or Reflection

1. What are your thoughts about the connections between studying the word of God and seeking God in prayer? What pattern does Daniel exhibit in the collocation of these two avenues of study for our successful knowledge of the future?

2. What do you think of the three negative purposes of the prophecy on the seventy weeks? Have these purposes been fulfilled since Daniel's day?

3. What do you think you can see what the three positive purposes of the seventy weeks refers to? Have any of these purposes been fulfilled yet?

4. What horrible acts will the future antichrist do that Jesus also warned us about?

5. Are we as readers supposed to understand a prophecy such as this one on the seventy weeks? What did Jesus say on this same topic?

Preparing for a Time of Distress and Divine Deliverance

Daniel 10:1–21; 11:1–45; 12:1–13

The last three chapters of Daniel together form one final vision, yet it can easily be called the most complete revelation Daniel received. These chapters focus on the pressure two nations would place on Israel, but the twelfth chapter assures us Israel will be delivered in that final hour.

Daniel's final vision begins with a heading that serves as the date-formula for the chapter, just as it also appeared in 1:1, 2:1, 7:1, 8:1 and 9:1. The date was "the third year of Cyrus, king of Persia," which would place this vision almost three years after the vision in 9:1, which took place in the "first year of Darius." This would then place it as late as 536 B.C.E. So, if Daniel entered Babylonian civil service about 606 or 605, then the third year of Cyrus would have marked the end of the seventy years of captivity in Babylon, the same period the prophet Jeremiah noted this exile would last for those seventy years (25:11–12; 29:10).

Already, two years earlier, a small group had gone back to Jerusalem and attempted to rebuild the temple under the leadership of Ezra, but a work stoppage had halted that effort because of opposition from the returnees' own people in Jerusalem. Whether Daniel was still working in a public office, we do not know for sure, yet Daniel 1:21 suggests Daniel held office at least until the first year of Cyrus.

The four visions that make up the final part of Daniel (chapters 7–12) fall into a chronological order, as did the narratives of chapters 1–

6. Thus, chapters 7 and 8 came in the first and third years of Belshazzar's reign, which belong chronologically between the events recorded in chapters 4 and 5 in the narrative section. Likewise, chapters 9 and 10–12 came in the first and third years of Cyrus's reign, so they came later than the events mentioned in the narratives in 1–6.

The last three chapters of Daniel, broadly speaking, fall into a three-part structure: (1) a prologue in 10:1–19, (2) a report of the vision in 10:20–12:4 and (3) an epilogue in 12:5–13.

The Vision From the Heavenly Messenger – 10:1–11:1

The Vision on the Banks of the Tigris – 10:1–4

The opening verse is narrated in the third person, while the vision itself is in the first person. The narrator introduced the content of this vision as a "revelation" (Hebrew *galah*), i.e., an "uncovering" or "disclosure" from God to his servant Daniel. But this revelation was as much a "word" from God as well, for the narrator also called it a "message" (Hebrew *dabar*, "word," which came to him in a "vision" (Hebrew *mar'eh*, 10:1), i.e., it was what could be "seen" as a word as well from God. The message itself "concerned a great war" (10:1), but no more information is given later about this point.

Some commentators note that Daniel's date-formulas cluster in the first three years of a king, which suggests God was seen to be Lord even in the key transitions (usually the most sensitive of times) in history. Thus, this fourth vision came three years after the revelation of the vision of the "seventy 'sevens'" in chapter 9.

King Cyrus had entered the city of Babylon as a new conqueror in October of 539 and established himself as the head of the Medo-Persian Empire. One of his first edicts came in March of 538, when he permitted captive groups, whom the Babylonians had taken from their homelands, to go back home to their Gentile countries. This release also applied to the Jewish people, though they are not explicitly mentioned on the "Cyrus cylinder," an archaeological artifact that more fully describes this edict. But Daniel remained behind in the land of captivity, as the listing of his Babylonian name, Belteshazzar, would remind him and us (10:1). Thus, within the year, Sheshbazzar (Ezra 1:1–4, 11; the same person as Governor Zerubbabel), who led some of the Hebrew captives back home and where he rebuilt the sacrificial altar (Ezra 3: 1-3). The returnees proceeded to lay the foundation footers for building this second temple in April of 536, but that effort was soon abandoned and left uncompleted for sixteen years, due to deep division between the younger generation and the older folks, who had seen the (First) Solomonic Temple, whose ancient foundational footprint compared magnificently better to this much-smaller footprint of the proposed new temple (Ezra 4:1, 24). The oldsters, after seeing the smaller layout of the footprint for the new temple, thought the time was not a right time for such a project. But the younger generation was so glad to see something underway by way of a temple that they rejoiced that the project was started; but because of the discord over the smaller projected building, the work came to an abrupt halt for sixteen years!

The message that Daniel now received, however, was so heavy that he fasted for "three weeks" (v. 2), cutting out all "choice food," all meat and wine; and he used "no lotions" until the three weeks were over (v. 3). The rejection of lotions may seem easy enough until we recall that the climate was desert-like, so it was necessary to lubricate the skin in such low humidity. Ordinarily, this time would have included festal anointing with oil as an indication of one's joy and gladness at a festival time. But now the times were different!

Daniel found himself standing on the banks of the Tigris River (v. 4) at the time of the feasts of the Passover and Unleavened Bread (cf. Lev. 23:5), which also fell "on the twenty-fourth day of the first month" (v. 4a). The mighty Tigris was some 1150 miles long, but 500 miles shorter than the Euphrates on the east side of Babylon. Just why he was on the banks of the Tigris at that time, he does not say. Was it government business, or was he there just for some seclusion and rest?

The Man in Linen at the Tigris River – 10:5–9

Daniel "looked up, and there before [him] was a man dressed in linen" (v. 5a). Linen was the traditional dress for Israel's priests (Exod. 28:5, 39, 42), but it also signified purity (28:42). The prophet Ezekiel also had seen an angel similarly dressed in linen (Ezek. 9:2–3), and angels clothed in bright linen also appear in the New Testament (Rev. 15:6). But was this man an angel, or even the interpreting angel Gabriel, who had appeared to Daniel earlier (8:16, 9:21)?

However, as the description of this "man" exceeds all ordinary angels, and as he shares features with the "Son of Man" in Revelation 1:13–16, I favor this being a Christophany instead of an angel. Daniel called this a "great vision" (v. 8a) for this very reason. Here are the four features in common with the "Son of Man" in Revelation 1:13–16: "A belt of the finest gold around his waist" (v. 5b) is like "a golden sash around his chest" (Rev. 1:13c). "His eyes [were] like flaming torches" (v. 6c) is like "his eyes were like blazing fire" (Rev. 1:14c). His "legs like the gleam of burnished bronze" (v. 6d) is like "his feet were like bronze glowing in a furnace" (Rev. 1:15a). And "His voice like the sound of a multitude" (v. 6e) is like "his voice was like the sound of rushing waters" (Rev. 1:15b).

This one who appeared to Daniel was a "man" (v. 5a, cf. 7:13–14), who was distinguished from the archangel Michael in 12:6–7. Thus, note the progress in revelation to Daniel from an interpreted dream to the highest form of revelation, viz., to the Second Person of the Trinity himself. We have already commented on his linen garment and the fact that his waist had a belt of gold from Uphaz, which may be the same place as Ophir. Therefore, when Near Eastern people went for a walk, or on a trip, they pulled up their long outer garment to their chest and belted it in their waist to hold the long garment up. Also, his body was like "chrysolite" or topaz (v. 6a), and his face was like "lightning" (v. 6b). His eyes were more like "flaming torches," while his arms and legs gleamed like burnished bronze" (v. 6d). When he spoke, it had the sound of a multitude (v. 6e). This surely must be a depiction of the pre-incarnate Messiah who came to strengthen Daniel in his weakness after he was weakened from seeing the vision.

Daniel says he was "the only one who saw the vision; those who were with me did not see it, but such terror overwhelmed them that they fled and hid themselves" (v. 7). Thus, he was left alone to gaze at this vision, but it had a devastating effect on him, so that he had no strength left (v. 8). As the Son of Man spoke to him, Daniel fell into a deep sleep with his face to the ground (v. 9). He had had a similar reaction to a vision previously when Gabriel came to interpret a vision (8:17).

Explaining to Daniel Future Happenings to Israel – 10:10–11:1

The hand that touched him (v. 10a) is not identified, but Yeshua would not need help from the angel Michael (v. 13), who appears elsewhere—10:21, 12:1; Jude 9; Revelation 12:7, and possibly 1 Thessalonians 4:16. But whoever touched Daniel, he got him up with his trembling hands and knees to a standing position, while the one touching him asserted that Daniel was indeed "highly esteemed" (vv. 10–11; cf. 9:23). Daniel stood there still trembling as he was assured that this one had been sent to speak these words to him, and he was to consider carefully what was said (v. 11). His experience of being touched on the lips is reminiscent of Isaiah's throne vision, wherein a live coal was taken from the altar by an angelic being to purify his lips (Isa. 6:6–7). But Daniel was not asking for purification; he was asking for strength.

This one explained to Daniel why he had been tardy, for the words of Daniel's prayers had been heard ever since the first day he had started praying (v. 12). The answer was delayed because "the prince of the Persian kingdom" had resisted this messenger for "twenty-one days" (v. 13). But Daniel was not to be afraid, for God still wanted to show this "highly esteemed" man his divine favor.

This prince of the Persian kingdom is presented not as a patron, but as an evil angel, one that exercised some sort of power over the Persian Empire as a delegate of Satan. That is an interesting piece of divine teaching about human governments. The reality of evil angels is set forth in Scripture in passages like 2 Peter 2:4 and Jude 6. In other places, the Bible makes a link between dumb idols and demons (Deut. 32:17; Ps. 106:37–38; 1 Cor. 10:20). One thing is clear: There is a spiritual battle going on in this world between good and evil. The evil angel hampered the message reaching Daniel about what would happen to his people Israel in the future (v. 14). Thus, Daniel he was given an insight into the spiritual conflict being fought, a battle to hinder the cause and the explanation from God from reaching him. Nowhere does that conflict reach higher stakes than when Satan's kingdom is confronted by the Kingdom of God and its involvement with the people of Israel.

Daniel was still in the throes of his spiritual and emotional struggle that continued to render him "speechless" (v. 15) by all this talk about a celestial warfare somewhere over the skies of Persia, yet it had a real impact on the work of human government!

Daniel needed a second touch for added strength. He was told, "Do not be afraid. … Peace! Be strong now; be strong" (v. 19). Once again, his visitor asked, "Do you know why I have come to you?" (v. 20a). The visitor had to return to fight with the prince of Persia, and when he left, the prince of Greece would come (v. 20b–c). But there was a matter of business that had to be dealt with first, before the Son of Man returned to the fray; he had to tell Daniel "What is written in the Book of Truth" (v. 21). This book, which was altogether reliable, contained the decisions and counsel of what would take place in the future. It was already written down (cf. Ps. 56:8; 130:16; Mal. 3:16). Since it is already recorded in God's book, history will proceed according to Scripture as God has purposed it. This fact only heightens the tragedy of critical scholars, who put Daniel in the Critics' Den and propose that these prophecies and predictions were mere fantasies. This history of Daniel was written in the second century B.C.E., yet according to the liberal view, the events it so accurately described had already happened.

The Prophecies About the Nations as They Prepare for the Final Conflict With Israel – 11:2–45

The Prophecy About Persia – 11:2

"Three more kings … then a fourth" does not mean three kings after Cyrus and then a fourth will come, for there were more than a total of five Persian rulers. However, in line with the idiom of the wisdom sayings, "for three, yea four" (the "x"+1 formula; e.g., Prov. 30:15–31; Amos 1–2), this would indicate the totality of examples covering all the Persian kings. Xerxes is the best candidate for this "fourth" king, since he was extremely wealthy, and had invaded Greece.

The Prophecy About Greece – 11:3–4

The "mighty king" mentioned here is undoubtedly Alexander the Great. He would come to the throne vacated by his father Phillip in 336. He did indeed "rule with great power" and he did, in fact, rule "as he please[d]." He appeared unstoppable in his military conquests. But at the height of his power and conquests, he died of a fever in Babylon in 323. So his empire was eventually divided between his four generals: Macedonia and Greece were given to Cassander; Thrace and Asia Minor (today Turkey) were given to Lysimachus; northern Syria, Mesopotamia and regions to the east were given to Seleucus, and southern Palestine and Egypt were given to Ptolemy. Thus the Greek Empire did "not go to [Alexander's] descendants" (v. 11:4b) but to his military generals.

The Prophecies About the Kings of the South and the North – 11:5–20

"The king of the South" (11:5), Ptolemy I Soter, son of Lagus, one of Alexander's generals, became governor of Egypt. He announced he was king of Egypt in 305, and he founded a long-lasting dynasty. But "one of his commanders" (11:5), Peridiccas, became regent until one of his generals, Seleucus, became part of a group that assassinated Peridiccas in 321. Seleucus gained control of Babylon but was forced to flee from Peridiccas's successor, Antigonus. Seleucus served as one of Ptolemy's generals from 316–312 as Ptolemy and Seleucus defeated Antigonus in the Battle of Gaza, leaving Seleucus free to regain Babylon once again. This started the battle between the Seleucids and the Ptolemies for control of Syria and Palestine—a battle that would last for two centuries.

Around 250, Ptolemy II made a treaty with Seleucus II by giving him his daughter Bernice in marriage ("the daughter of the king of the South," v. 6). Antiochus I (280–261) divorced his wife Laodice and disinherited his two sons by her, instead naming his new son by Bernice as the new inheritor of the throne. Two years later he was reconciled to Laodice, only to be poisoned just as Laodice poisoned Bernice, her son, and those associated with her. Since Bernice's father died before her murder, it was left to her brother, Ptolemy III (246–221 B.C.E.), of whom it was said, "One from her family line will arise," v. 7) to avenge Bernice's death. He invaded Syria, captured Antioch and Seleucia, and killed Laodice, but before he returned to Egypt to deal with trouble. Seleucus II (246–226), one of Laodice's brothers, regained control of Syria in the meantime.

In 242, Seleucus II tried to invade Egypt (v. :9), but he was forced to retreat. "His sons will prepare for war and assemble a great army"

(v. 10), thus Seleucus III (226–223) would succeed his father, but he was murdered during his campaign in Asia Minor in 223. His brother Antiochus III (223–187), with a large army, moved against Ptolemy IV (221–203), but Ptolemy met him with his own large army (v. 11) at Raphia in 217 and defeated him there. This victory put Palestine and much of Syria under Egyptian Ptolemaic control.

The king of the North mustered another huge army (v. 13) against the new Ptolemy V (203–181), who came to the throne at just six years old when his father died. At first the king of the North lost to Egyptian general Scopas at the Battle of Gaza, but he won at the Battle of Panelas/Banias in 200, where the source of the Jordan is found south of Mount Hermon. From this time on, the Seleucids held control of Palestine and Syria.

Daniel was also told that "violent men among your own people will rebel" (v. 14b), likely referring to the same incident mentioned by Josephus (*Antiquities* 12.3.3–4), in which the Jewish people did not take too kindly to the Ptolemaic side, but when the Seleucid factions visited Jerusalem, they were well-received, for they promised to give the Jews the freedom to live by their own ancestral rules.

Later, the king of the North, Antiochus, captured the city of Sidon (v. 15), to which Scopus and his Egyptian army had retreated after their defeat at Paneas. When the Seleucid siege led to a famine in 198, the king of the South surrendered. This Egyptian surrender finally settled Antiochus III's control of Syria and Palestine; as Daniel 11:16 affirmed, "He will establish himself in the Beautiful Land."

Because of the growing power of the Romans, Antiochus gave his daughter Cleopatra for a wife to Ptolemy V (203–181 B.C.E.; v. 17c, "He will give him a daughter in marriage in order to overthrow the kingdom, but his plans will not succeed or help him"). Whereas he had hoped that she would act as a spy, instead she became loyal to her husband and urged him to form an alliance with Rome.

"He will turn his attention to the coastlands and will take many of them" (v. 18). Thus, Antiochus took over the Egyptian-held coast of Asia Minor and moved to seize the Macedonian possessions of Thrace. However, "a commander will put an end to his insolence" (v. 18b). Antiochus invaded these areas in 192, but despite warnings from Rome, he proceeded to be crushed, first at the Battle of Thermopylae, and then at the Battle of Magnesia in 190. As a result, Antiochus became a vassal of Rome and with heavy indemnity; thus, he was left short of honor and funds. Daniel had also predicted Antiochus would "stumble and fall, to be seen no more" (v. 19b), for Antiochus and his men were assassinated by the local people as they tried to rob the temple of Bel in Elymais, Persia, to secure desperately needed funds to pay tribute to Rome.

Antiochus III had two sons: one was a hostage in Rome, and the other succeeded him as Seleucus IV (187–175). The story of what happened to Seleucus IV is contained in the apocryphal book of 3 Maccabees. He sent his prime minister Heliodorus to strip the funds in the Jerusalem temple, but he claimed he was prevented from doing so by a divine apparition that almost cost him his life. Seleucus was assassinated in 175 in a plot hatched by Heliodorus, as v. 20 predicted.

The Prophecy About the Last King of the South – 11:21–35

Commentators, whether of Jewish, Catholic or Protestant stripe, agree on the interpretation of this chapter through verse 20, but not from verse 21 onward. Most interpreters identify the "contemptible person" in v. 21–35 as Antiochus Epiphanes (175–164; "Epiphanes" means "the manifest," later scornfully nicknamed "Epimanes," meaning "madman," who is also the "little horn" in chapter 8. Some, such as Keil, think Antiochus Epiphanes IV is primarily represented in these verses, but typically they also point to the future antichrist. A better view is that the predictions in verses 21–35 refer directly to

Antiochus, but verses 36–45 directly refer to the future "antichrist" of the last days.

Antiochus' route to the throne is unclear, but he assumed the throne under the pretense of ruling on behalf of his nephew, who had been taken as a hostage to Rome. Following Antiochus III's policy of letting the Jews self-govern, the High Priest Onias III served as local ruler. But as he opposed the influx of Hellenization in Judea, Onias' brother Jason offered the king a huge sum of money as a bribe and promised to Hellenize Judea for him. But in 172, a man named Menelaus, not from a priestly family, offered an even larger bribe, so he replaced Jason. This is what "a prince of the covenant" (vv. 22–24) refers to, for Menelaus lured Jason from the temple and murdered him in 171.

Antiochus IV set out to invade Egypt (v. 25). He successfully captured Pelusium and Memphis, though not Alexandria. Antiochus IV made an alliance with Ptolemy VI (181–146), but Ptolemy was encouraged to attack Palestine; this provoked Antiochus to attack Egypt. On his return from Egypt, he raided the temple treasury in Jerusalem.

Egypt appealed to Rome for help (v. 30, "Ships of the western coastlands will oppose him, and he will lose heart"), so Antiochus was confronted near Alexandria and turned away from Egypt. He took out his anger on Jerusalem and made an edict proscribing all Jewish religious practices, including the observance of the Sabbath, offering sacrifices, or observing food laws and festivals on pain of death (v. 31). He also set up the "abomination that causes desolation" (v. 31b), which 1 Maccabees 1:54 says that on the 15th of Chislev, 167 B.C.E., an altar was erected, which was an idol of Zeus.

One Jewish family particularly objected to this sacrilege—a priest named Mattathias, along with his five children. One son in particular, Judas Maccabeus (meaning "[the] hammer"), inflicted defeats on the

Syrian forces. Three years after the desecration of the temple (December 164), Judas regained control of Jerusalem, purified the temple, and resumed sacrifices.

The Prophecy of the Willful King – 11:36–45

Whether Amillennial, Postmillennial or Premillennial, most interpreters agree that the final ten verses of chapter 11 point to the general character, person, and career of the antichrist of the end-times. The context for this event is in the last days as Daniel 10:14 sets this vision: "the vision concerns a time yet to come." Moreover, the behavior of the "little horn" of Daniel 7:24, 2 Thessalonians 2:3 ("the man of lawlessness") and the "beast" of Revelation 13:1 is so strikingly similar that these texts must all refer to the same king who will appear in the last days.

"He will show no respect for the gods of his fathers … nor will he regard any god but will exalt himself above them all" (v. 37), just as the beast in Revelation 13:6 opens his mouth "to blaspheme God and to slander his name and his dwelling place." Indeed, he "will exalt himself above all," exactly as 2 Thess. 2:4 says of the man of lawlessness, who "will exalt himself over everything that is called God or is worshiped."

But this antichrist will meet his end after a time of success, but then the "time of wrath" will come (vv. 36, 40, 45), when three momentous events occur: the great tribulation of Israel, the resurrection of the dead and the final reward of the righteous (12:1–3).

This prophecy of the antichrist shifts from this history of the contemptible personage of Antiochus IV to the final appearance of the new antichrist. Comprehended in the image of the king, who historically was typified in Antiochus, was the prediction of the future antichrist, who would completely fulfill all that was predicted in one prophetic oracle. Since nothing in history can be identified as corresponding to verses 36–45, it is proper to look to the future for their fulfillment.

The Prophecies About Israel at the End of Time – 12:1–13

Some of the predictions about the antichrist are: (1) "He will also invade the Beautiful Land" (11:41), the land of Israel; (2) "There will be a time of distress such as has not happened from the beginning of the nations until then" (12:1b); and (3) there will be "multitudes who sleep in the dust of the earth [who] will awake, some to everlasting life, others to shame and everlasting contempt" (v. 2)—a resurrection of two kinds of the dead to two kinds of everlasting life.

The Great Tribulation – 12:1

This means Israel will certainly by this time have been restored to the land of Palestine as had been promised to them so frequently throughout Scripture. But the antichrist will seek to destroy Israel as he invades the "glorious land" and plants "his royal tents of his palace between the seas [the Mediterranean Sea and the Dead Sea] at the beautiful holy mountain" (11:45). Despite all this effort, "he will come to his end, and no one will help him" (v. 45b). Further information on his failure is explained by the missionary Paul in 2 Thessalonians 2:2 and by the Apostle John in Revelation 19:11–21. 12:1 describes the conditions of those final days under the antichrist. The references to Israel in are real; there is no reason to transfer these references over to the Church in a type of replacement or supersessionist theology.

The Resurrection of the Dead – 12:2

Verse 2 tells of physical resurrection. Those who spiritualize or find symbols of something other than a physical resurrection miss the meaning of this passage. There are two separate resurrections at two separate times: one to everlasting life to be with the Lord, and the other raised briefly to answer why they had never received Jesus as

Lord and Savior, only to be cast out into hell and dwell there forever. Thus, two physical resurrections are noted.

The order of the resurrections is taught in Scripture as follows: (1) Messiah was the first one to be raised from the dead physically, (2) those who belong to Messiah by faith will be raised in connection with his second coming, and finally (3) all those remaining who have not put their trust in Messiah will be raised to face the judgment of the "great white throne" at the end of Messiah's millennial reign (1 Cor. 15:22–28; John 5:28) and face their eternal judgment.

The Final Reward of the Just – 12:3

Daniel closes his book with a promise to those who are wise: They "will shine like the brightness of the heavens," and "those who lead many to righteousness [will] be like the stars for ever and ever" (v. 3).

The Disposition of These Prophetic Words – 12:4–13

As Daniel looked up, there stood two others, one on this bank on this side of the river and the other one on the opposite bank (v. 5). The one clothed in linen said that all these things would be completed in 3½ years when the power of the holy people [of Israel] had been broken (v. 7). Daniel was to go on his way because the words would be fulfilled in their time (vv. 9, 13). God would see to that! What a great promise to end a magnificent book!

Conclusions

1. God has spoken so accurately and with such detail that few have missed what was said about the kings of the North and South. Instead, critical scholars have turned the interpretation around and said someone claiming to be Daniel authored this book after these events happened but worded it in such a way that it was a prediction in each case.

2. Few Old Testament passages are clearer about the resurrection of the righteous being separate from the later resurrection of the unjust. However, all will be resurrected in their specified times to face the Lord, some to everlasting life and some to eternal torment.

3. The antichrist is a major figure who will appear in the last days, but his end will be sure and sudden.

4. Jesus is the Lord of all history and knows exactly where it is going.

Questions for Discussion or Reflection

1. What is your estimate of who the man clothed in linen is? What arguments can you give for your conclusions?

2. Why does our Lord give such an enormous amount of detail for the successor of the kings of the North and the South? Of what use are these details?

3. Why does the description of Antiochus Epiphanes IV lead into a description of the antichrist of the final days? How are they alike? In what ways do they differ?

4. How does Daniel distinguish between the two resurrections in chapter 12? Where else in Scripture can you get just as clear a picture of this separation? and what elements do they share, and what elements are different?

Excursus

"Darius the Mede"

As this book was going to press, I received the superb article by Rodger C. Young, "How Darius the Mede Was Deleted From History and Who Did It" in *Bible and Spade* magazine (35.3, 4, Summer/Fall 2022, 28–33). Young noted, as we have already indicated, that Liberal scholarship has been skeptical of many facts in Daniel, but especially that there was such a man as "Darius the Mede" who ever existed. For example, Dr. John J. Collins wrote: "No such person as Darius the Mede is known to have existed apart from the narrative of Daniel. The Babylonian Empire did not fall to the Medes but to the Persians."

However, Young made a rather convincing case for the fact that just as there had been an attempt to expunge King Belshazzar's name from the record of Babylonian kings in deference to his father Nabonidus, so an even more successful propogandist attempt was made against recognizing Darius the Mede as one of the two conquerors of Babylon and eradicating his name from the historical record in favor of Cyrus the Persian for propogandist's reasons.

Young's article points to an early third century B.C.E. source, a Chaldean historian named Berossus, whose work survives in extracts found in the Esagila Temple in Babylon and also in Josephus' work *Against Apion* (1:153) and in the Armenian translation of Eusebius' *Chronicle* that it was Darius the Mede who reigned superbly after the Fall of Babylon for the conquering Medes and Persians for a short time before his death. The Cyropedia (8.7.1) suggested that Cyaxerxes II enjoyed a notably short reign in 539 B.C.E. (cf. Dan. 5:31; 9:1; 10:1; 11:1), dying within two years after the Fall of Babylon in October 539. Thus, there was a real Cyaxerxes II, whose throne name (many kings of the era used a dual name) was Darius the Mede. So, there was a real Darius the Mede, whose name and work is not to be confused with the later Darius Hystaspes, who reigned from 522 to 486.

There is much more to this story, but I wanted to update what had been said in my comments, for they are crucial to the long debate over the name of Darius the Mede.

The Lives and Ministries of ELIJAH and ELISHA
PRAYING LIKE THE JEW JESUS
His Names Are Wonderful
Barbara D. Malda   Come and Worship
Under THE FIG TREE   PATRICK GABRIEL LUMBROSO
Under THE VINE   PATRICK GABRIEL LUMBROSO
Making Eye Contact with God
You Bring the Bagels I'll Bring the Gospel   RUBIN
THE WORLD TO COME   LEMAN
Psalms & Proverbs   David H. Stern
MESSIANIC JUDAISM   STERN
GOD's APPOINTED CUSTOMS   KASDAN
GOD's APPOINTED TIMES   KASDAN
Passover
GATEWAYS TO TORAH   RABBI RUSSELL RESNIK
CREATION to COMPLETION   RESNIK
Is Christ Really The End of The Law?
To the Ends of the Earth
On The Way to Emmaus   Dr. Jacques Doukhan
YESHUA
JEWISH NEW TESTAMENT COMMENTARY
MATTHEW PRESENTS YESHUA, KING MESSIAH   KASDAN

Printed in the United States
by Baker & Taylor Publisher Services